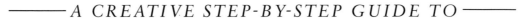

A CREATIVE STEP-BY-STEP GUIDE TO

GROWING
PERENNIALS

A CREATIVE STEP-BY-STEP GUIDE TO

GROWING
PERENNIALS

Author
Sue Phillips

Photographer
Neil Sutherland

COOMBE BOOKS

4539
This edition published in 1998 by Coombe Books
© 1998 Quadrillion Publishing Limited,
Godalming, Surrey GU7 1XW, England
Printed and bound in Singapore
ISBN 1-85833-884-0

Credits
Edited, designed and typeset by Ideas into Print
Photographs: Neil Sutherland
Production: Neil Randles, Karen Staff

THE AUTHOR

Sue Phillips After leaving school, Sue Phillips worked for a year on a general nursery before studying horticulture at Hadlow College of Agriculture and Horticulture, Kent for three years. For the next five years, she was co-owner and manager of a nursery in Cambridgeshire before joining a leading garden products company as Garden Adviser. This involved answering gardening queries, handling complaints, writing articles and press releases, speaking at gardening events and broadcasting for local radio. In 1984, Sue turned freelance and since then has written several books, contributed widely to various gardening and general interest magazines and appeared often on radio and TV.

THE PHOTOGRAPHER

Neil Sutherland has more than 30 years experience in a wide range of photographic fields, including still-life, portraiture, reportage, natural history, cookery, landscape and travel. His work has been published in countless books and magazines throughout the world.

Half-title page: The flowers and foliage of Helianthus *'Lemon Queen', bring color and interest to the late-season garden. This compact cultivar grows 5ft(1.5m) tall.*
Title page: Summer and fall perennials provide a dazzling array of flower shapes and textures in the garden. Many can also be cut and enjoyed in the home.
Copyright page: The candelabra primulas, P. bulleyana *and* P. beesiana, *hybridize to produce this strikingly colored* Primula x bulleesiana. *Like other similar primulas, this one will flourish in damp soil and along the edges of streams.*

CONTENTS

FASHIONABLE AND VERSATILE PLANTS

As their name suggests, perennials are plants that live for many years. But unlike woody plants – trees, shrubs and climbers – herbaceous perennials (known as perennials for short) have soft stems that die down each fall. The plants spend the winter resting underground as dormant roots, then burst back to life in a rush of new growth the following spring.

Years ago, it was difficult to find more than a few basic perennial varieties on sale, but now they are the rapidly rising stars of gardening fashion, stocked everywhere in a bewildering array. You can choose old favorites or the latest new varieties fresh from the breeders; rare and antique plants to be treasured and cosseted, or rampaging spreaders that fill the space fast. You can choose between hot strong colors and bold striking shapes, or softer pastels and gentle shapes that blend together to make a floral tapestry. Perennials are endlessly versatile, and bring variety and interest to the garden as the pattern of flowers in bloom at any time changes continually with the seasons. And although they certainly need a bit more work than a garden of evergreen shrubs, perennials do not take a great deal of effort to care for and amply repay their keep. They are still used in the traditional way, in formal herbaceous borders or in mixed borders between shrubs and trees, but now perennials are also very popular for growing in containers on the patio, in flowering meadows, bog gardens, rock features and beside ponds. There are so many different kinds to choose from, for both sunny and shady situations and for all soil types, that there truly is a perennial for every place in the garden.

*Left: Lupins are superb perennials. **Right:** Geranium himalayense 'Gravetye'.*

11

What is a perennial?

Herbaceous perennials are plants that grow and flower in one season, then die down and spend the winter as dormant roots and reappear the following spring. There are all shapes and sizes, from giants, such as gunnera, to low ground-coverers, such as pulmonaria. Some, such as these two examples, may be grown as much for their foliage as their flowers. However, nurserymen often categorize certain low evergreen plants, such as hellebores and *Alchemilla mollis,* as perennials, along with the evergreen species of euphorbia and ornamental grasses. Even agapanthus and lilies can count as perennials as they die down in winter and are left in the same spot for many years. By perennials, we usually mean plants of sufficient size and a suitable constitution for growing in beds and borders. (Very small perennials, particularly those needing very well-drained conditions, are usually classed as rock plants.) Despite the botanical boundaries, all the types of plants loosely known as perennials are grown in much the same way as herbaceous perennials and fit well into herbaceous planting schemes.

Left: Euphorbia griffithii 'Fireglow' has bright flowers in early summer; it retains its decorative foliage and red stems for the entire growing season.

Below: Verbena bonariensis *is quite shortlived, particularly on heavy clay or in cold winters, but plants usually seed themselves and replace losses.*

Below: Lilies are traditionally grown in herbaceous borders for their large trumpet-shaped summer flowers, which complement the classic spire shapes of many favorite perennials.

Lupin

Left: Even after the flowers are over, iris are valuable for their spear-shaped foliage. Bearded iris are evergreen, but most other types die down in winter, including this Iris sibirica.

Right: You can buy perennials as small plants and enjoy watching them grow into splendid specimens in your garden. Even at this young stage, you can recognize the foliage shapes typical of the mature plants.

Erigeron

Delphinium

Buying perennials

Because true perennials die down in winter, the best time to buy plants is in spring, when a few shoots have appeared, so that it is obvious that you are not buying an empty pot of soil. Perennials can also be planted during the growing season. Choose strong, healthy-looking plants with rich green leaves or plump growth buds. Avoid any with pale or sickly foliage, or those that have been shredded by pests or are disfigured by reddish brown rust spots or other obvious disease symptoms. Weeds, moss or lichen in the pots may not be a problem, but might indicate that plants have been standing outside for a long time and may not have been fed.

Right: Grasses, such as this Hakonechloa macra 'Alboaurea', contrast well with other perennials. Some grasses are evergreen, but this species is a true perennial that dies down in winter.

Right: Penstemons are very drought-resistant and useful for hot sunny sites. However, they are not reliably winter hardy in cold areas, so overwinter cuttings under cover.

Hemerocallis (day lily)

Oriental poppy

Campanula persicifolia

Classic lupins

Lupins are classic herbaceous border plants, whose tall, elegant, spire-shaped flowers are available in a range of sensational two-tone colors. The foliage is unlike that of any other perennial, and makes a good secondary attraction. The variety shown on the left is Lupinus 'Poached Salmon'.

Right: At the end of the season, when the foliage starts to die back, cut herbaceous plants down to just above ground level.

The perennial year

In the past, when they were grown in fields and dug up from the nursery beds during the dormant season, perennials were sold for planting out in fall or spring. Today, perennials are usually sold in pots, which makes it safe to plant them later in spring or summer, even when they are in full flower. The advantage of doing this is that you get instant effect; you can put in a new plant to fill a gap in the border whenever you like, with no need to wait for the 'right' time of year. It also makes it possible to indulge in 'impulse buys' when visiting a garden center. Another advantage is that you do not have the worry associated with putting in a dormant plant; because you can see it growing, you know it is alive. The disadvantage of planting perennials while in growth is that, because the plant is in full leaf (and maybe even flower), it needs much more care to become established. The very best time for planting pot-grown perennials however is mid-spring. This way you can be sure of buying a live plant since new shoots will be appearing by then, but there is some time for new plants to become established before flowering.

Whenever you plant, good soil preparation is vital, as perennials will remain in the same ground for two to four years. If soil pests are a problem, tackle them in winter by digging the ground over several times to expose them to birds. Otherwise use a soil pesticide shortly before planting. Dig in plenty of well-rotted organic matter to help the soil hold moisture. On very dry sandy soils you could also fork in some water-retaining gel crystals, (as sold for hanging baskets) to help moisture retention. Conversely, on heavy clay soils, fork in coarse grit as well as organic matter to improve aeration and drainage. Sprinkle a general fertilizer evenly over the soil and rake it in shortly before planting. After planting, water well in and apply a thick mulch of garden compost, chipped bark or similar material to keep the soil moist around the roots. Continue to water newly planted perennials in dry weather for the remainder of their first summer.

Care calendar

Early spring: Lift and divide any congested perennials; weed and apply a 1-2in(2.5-5cm) mulch of well-rotted organic matter, chipped bark, etc., while the soil is moist.

Mid-spring: Put plant supports in place. Apply general-purpose fertilizer and water it in if the soil is dry. Repeat this six to eight weeks later. If granules of fertilizer become lodged in the crown of the plant or on foliage, wash it off straight away or it may scorch the plant and kill young growth.

Summer: Apply occasional half-strength liquid tomato feeds (high-potash) to encourage bud initiation and flowering. If any feed splashes onto the foliage, wash it off with a hose. Deadhead often to keep plants flowering as long as possible. Hoe or weed regularly to avoid plants being smothered.

Fall: Cut off dying foliage and stems close to the ground to tidy the border. Alternatively, leave seedheads for the birds and some stems at the backs of borders to house beneficial insects over winter. Protect the crowns of slightly frost-tender plants such as penstemon with a layer of evergreen prunings, hedge clippings or similar material. Protect gunnera by covering the crowns of the plants with a thick layer of their own dead leaves during the winter months.

Staking perennials

Perennials with frail slender stems or a sprawling habit need support to keep them in control. Position supports in spring when new growth is visible and not too tall.

Right: Place a 'grow-through' support over the plant's crown and adjust the grid to a suitable height. It will soon be hidden by foliage.

Left: Providing the support frame is not placed too high, plants soon grow through it. At 4-6in(10-15cm) below the usual bulk of foliage, the frame is still high enough to support the flower stems.

3 Sprinkle a handful of general-purpose fertilizer into the hole and mix well with the soil. Add half a handful of fertilizer to the pile of soil alongside the hole and, again, mix well.

1 Prepare the soil over the entire bed some time in advance of planting. Dig a hole for each plant about twice the size of the rootball.

2 Put the excavated soil next to the hole for filling in. Mix some well-rotted manure into the base of the hole; add more to the excavated soil.

4 Lift the plant by its rootball (not its stems) into the hole. The top of the rootball should be roughly level with the soil surface. Rotate the plant until its best side faces the front of the bed.

5 Surround the rootball with the improved soil excavated from the planting hole, and firm it down lightly. Add more soil to bring it up to the level of the surrounding bed.

6 Trickle water around the rootball until thoroughly wet. Mulch with 1-2in(2.5-5cm) of rotted organic matter or bark chips and keep well watered.

Above: Support bushy moundlike plants by pushing 24in(60cm)-long twiggy branches in round the crown of the plant in spring. They disappear among the shoots.

Left: Delphinium stems are best supported along their entire length by tying them loosely in several places to a tall cane. Green canes look the least obtrusive.

1 *In spring, a mature red hot poker plant looks very dilapidated, with many brown and dead leaves. This is a plant in need of rejuvenation and now is the time to divide it up, before it starts growing strongly. Division is also one of the best methods for propagating perennial plants.*

Dividing perennials

Perennial plants grow by sending out new shoots around the center of the plant, to make it spread. In time, the oldest shoots in the middle of clumps become exhausted, and this is the time to dig up and divide mature plants into smaller clumps. Throw away the oldest pieces from the center and only replant vigorous healthy new pieces taken from around the edges. The length of time before division is needed varies from one kind of perennial to another, and to some extent from one garden to another, as in some places plants grow faster than others. Be guided by the appearance of the plant; when the middle starts to die out, lack vigor, or produce only small, stunted leaves or shoots, make a mental note to lift and divide it at the next opportunity. Plants that have spread beyond acceptable boundaries may also be candidates for division, simply to restrict their run. As a general rule, fast-growing plants, such as Michaelmas daisies, may need dividing as often as every three years. Tough plants can be lifted and divided in the fall; divide choicer and more delicate kinds in spring, just as they start into growth. This avoids any risk that torn roots, damaged stems or open wounds may rot during cold damp winter weather.

2 *Dig a fork in close to the base of the plant to lever the clump out of the ground. Dig deeply to get as much of the root out as possible, and take care not to damage the stems.*

3 *As the clump emerges, you can see that it is made up of many smaller crowns pressed close together. When separated and given more space, they make good new plants.*

4 *After shaking as much soil as possible from the clump, start pulling it apart. Since red hot pokers are tough plants, this is not easy. Wear gardening gloves if handling a plant with sharp leaves.*

5 *With the old plant out of the way, take this opportunity to replenish the soil. Tip a bucket of organic matter and sprinkle a handful of general fertilizer over the spot.*

6 *Fork this well in; improve the soil whether you plant a new red hot poker in the same spot or intend putting in a different plant. Red hot pokers take a lot out of the ground.*

7 *Choose the best piece from the original clump to replant; ideally, this should have four or five good strong shoots, as here. Peel away any dead or broken leaves from the base, make a planting hole and sit the new plant in position.*

8 *Spread the roots well out in the base of the hole and fill in with topsoil. Mix some more organic matter in to improve this if necessary. Firm the soil gently with your heel to consolidate it round the roots, but do not overdo it.*

Above: *Kniphofia uvaria maxima makes an imposing clump with tall pokers up to 7ft(2.15m) high in mid- to late summer. Consider growing a clump as a specimen plant in a lawn.*

9 *The new plant will take a while to settle down and start growing again, but should make a well-shaped clump and start flowering again the following year. A large strong clump may even flower later the same year after division if it establishes quickly.*

Right: *'Percy's Pride' is a neat plant with short, tidy foliage and lime-cream pokers. It grows to about 36in(90cm) and like all the choice dwarf pokers, needs humus-rich, well-drained soil and a deep mulch in the fall to protect the plant in winter.*

Taking cuttings

Although virtually all perennials can be propagated by division, it is not always convenient. There may be times when you would like to give a friend a plant from the garden or you may want to propagate a plant that is too small to divide. You may simply have missed the right time of year for dividing something you want to make more of. In these cases, cuttings provide the simple solution. There are no rules about which plants must be propagated by any particular type of cutting; simply choose the easiest method. If possible, use Irishman's cuttings, as these give quicker and more reliable results. This way, you will also need to take fewer cuttings to ensure having at least one or two root. However, it is always a good idea to take two or three cuttings to allow for possible losses; if they all root, you can then select the strongest to plant. Better still, pot them all into one pot to produce a large plant much faster than usual – a useful tip if you need to produce plants in a hurry. When selecting material to take for cuttings, use non-flowering shoots if at all possible as they root much better than flowering ones. If it is not possible to find a non-flowering shoot, take a strong flowering one, but remove the growing tip along with any buds or flowers to reduce water loss.

Basal cuttings

Use this technique to propagate many kinds of herbaceous plants in spring, as soon as the new stems are big enough to use as cuttings. Usually 2-4in(5-10cm) is all you need.

1 *In early spring, choose a strong shoot arising from the very base of the plant and cut it off below ground level with a sharp knife. The white part of the stem below ground produces better roots.*

Irishman's cuttings

The stems of clump-forming plants such as aster make a few wispy roots while still attached to the parent. Use these for propagation.

1 *Clear the soil from the edge of the plant and select a plump shoot that already has small roots. Detach the stem with its roots.*

2 *Loosely fill a 3.5in(9cm) pot with seed mix and make a deep hole in the middle so that all the roots can spread out. Lower the plant carefully, allowing the roots to go in straight.*

3 *Firm in gently so that the plant stays upright and the seed mixture is consolidated around the roots. Although partly rooted, Irishman's cuttings are quite fragile at this stage.*

4 *Water in lightly, then place in a propagator or a loosely tied plastic bag. Shade lightly and keep the mix just moist. Signs of new growth should appear in 4-6 weeks.*

Encouraging cuttings to root

After taking cuttings, give them shady conditions to root. You may choose to reserve a corner of the garden, with perhaps a cold frame whose glass has been replaced by shading fabric, for propagation. Alternatively, root cuttings in a cool shady part of the greenhouse or at a window indoors where they get some light but are out of direct sun. Put pots of cuttings into a large loose plastic bag to keep them humid until they start rooting. Once rooted, pot up cuttings taken in spring and summer, one per pot, and grow them on in nursery conditions until they are big enough to plant out in the garden – usually the following spring. Leave cuttings taken in late summer and early fall in their original pots until the following spring, and then repot them. They will be ready to plant out later in the summer.

Spring
Take basal cuttings of cranesbills, delphiniums, lupins and scabious.

Spring and summer
Take Irishman's cuttings of achillea, ajuga, Japanese anemones, anthemis, aster, campanula, hardy chrysanthemums, heuchera, nepeta, phlox and pyrethrum.

Summer and early fall
Take softwood cuttings in summer of nepeta, penstemon, phygelius, perennial salvias and zauschneria. Take softwood cuttings of pinks in midsummer just after flowering or use non-flowering shoots.

2 *Cleanly trim off the base of the cutting with a sharp knife to remove any torn or bruised tissue at the base of the stem. Use the knife so that it does not cut down onto your thumb, or cut down onto a board.*

3 *Remove the leaves from the bottom 1-2in(2.5-5cm) of stem. Cut them flush with the stem, leaving no ragged tissue that may cause the cutting to rot instead of root.*

4 *Dip the base of the cutting into hormone rooting powder to encourage rooting. The powder also contains fungicide, which helps prevent rotting. Replace rooting powder every spring.*

5 *Firm the cutting in gently with your fingertips and water it thoroughly. Stand the cuttings in a propagating case or in a loosely tied plastic bag to keep the air around them humid until they start rooting.*

If leaves dry out, the cutting is placed under stress and is less likely to root.

Planning a border

1 Start with 'key' plants – the tallest or most striking in the scheme. These should go towards the back of a traditional border, but avoid putting them in a straight line.

In large borders, put in upright plants in groups of three or five to make more impact.

2 Add medium-sized plants, so that they are not directly in front of the taller plants but appear staggered when the border is viewed from the front

3 Keep the shortest plants for the front to create a 'tiered' display that allows every plant to be seen instead of being swamped by its neighbors. Aim to achieve a harmonious blend of colors throughout, without one color dominating the others.

Traditional herbaceous borders are long, formal, rectangular beds in front of a hedge. They are used only for herbaceous perennials so that the flowering season is confined to summer. A traditional border needs a lot of maintenance, since the shade from the hedge causes many plants to grow weak stems that need supporting, and weeding is difficult as beds are often too wide to reach without treading on the soil. Today, mixed borders are much more practical, especially in small gardens. By planting perennials with spring bulbs, shrubs and even a few small ornamental trees, the bed provides year-round interest yet involves much less work. However, it is possible to create the formal look of a traditional border without the problems, by making a double border – a pair of matching formal rectangular borders with a path between them. This makes an attractive feature to divide a large lawn, and turns a functional path into a floral walk. Alternatively, add pergola poles and grow climbers above shade-tolerant herbaceous plants.
By keeping the border fairly narrow, weeds can easily be hoed out from either side, and since the bed is open on all sides only the tallest plants will need staking.

Key to plant names

1. Echinops ritro
2. Sidalcea *'Rose Queen'*
3. Thalictrum delavayi *'Hewitt's Double'*
4. Lupinus *Russell Hybrids*
5. Acanthus spinosus
6. Phlox paniculata *'Franz Schubert'*
7. Delphinium *Black Knight Group*
8. Hemerocallis *'Mallard'*
9. Cimicifuga simplex *'White Pearl'*
10. Salvia x sylvestris *'Indigo'*
11. Delphinium *Black Knight Group*
12. Crocosmia *x* crocosmiflora *'Emily McKenzie'*
13. Achillea *'Gold Plate'*
14. Lupinus *Russell Hybrids*
15. Campanula latifolia
16. Echinacea purpurea *'Robert Bloom'*
17. Monarda *'Prairie Night'*
18. Lamium maculatum *'Pink Pewter'*
19. Geranium pratense *'Mrs Kendall Clark'*
20. Prunella grandiflora *'Pink Loveliness'*
21. Persicaria bistorta *'Superba'*
22. Polemonium caeruleum *Brise d'Anjou*
23. Rudbeckia fulgida *'Goldsturm'*
24. Achillea *'Moonshine'*
25. Hosta *'Royal Standard'*
26. Stachys byzantina *'Primrose Heron'*
27. Polemonium caeruleum *Brise d'Anjou*
28. Prunella grandiflora *'Pink Loveliness'*
29. Aster *x* frikartii
30. Stachys lanata
31. Platycodon grandiflorus mariesii
32. Nepeta *'Six Hills Giant'*
33. Sedum atuntsuense *'Autumn Joy'*

Above: *In a well-planned border, you can mix many shades by arranging plants so that violently clashing colors are not placed next to each other, and by using foliage or pastels to damp down the effect of strong bright colors.*

Move 'plants' around until you are happy with the effect before starting to strip turf, prepare soil and plant.

Below: *When planning a complete new border from scratch, it is best to start with a 3D plan using 'models' to give an idea of the height, spread and color of each plant. You can make you own from styrofoam, using plant sizes gleaned from a nursery catalog or reference book.*

An island bed

1 *Start by placing the tallest, most striking plants in the center. This bed is based on 'hot' reds, oranges and yellows, with cream and purple foliage plants for contrast.*

2 *Place medium-sized plants around the tall central ones, but do not worry too much about making 'tiers', as the bed can be viewed from many angles and should look very informal.*

The foliage of flowering plants will also help to avoid the impression of solid color you get from a model.

3 *When working with a limited color scheme, as here, use paler shades to break up large blocks of strong color.*

Island beds are informally shaped beds cut out of a lawn, in which flowers are seen surrounded by a green grassy backdrop. You can walk all round them, enjoying the display from different angles. They are a useful way of planning a garden so you do not see everything from the house. The big advantage of island beds over traditional herbaceous borders is that plants receive light from all sides, so they grow shorter, stronger stems that need less support. Pests are much less of a problem when beds are surrounded by lawn than when backed by a hedge or fence, which harbors slugs and snails. Shapes should be gently curving and natural-looking. In an undulating garden, island beds look best fitted into natural depressions or carved like terraces into the sides of a gentle slope. On level ground, teardrop shapes look good. The beds should look in scale with the surrounding garden and house; in a large area, several island beds may look better than a large single one. Try to make shapes that 'interlock', with wide grass paths between them.

When choosing plants for an island bed, remember that they will be viewed from all round, so they need to complement all of their neighbors not just those immediately in front of and behind them. The easiest way to create good plant groupings is to stand plants together at the garden center before you buy them to judge the effect. When using a limited color scheme, such as red, orange and yellow, be sure to include plenty of good foliage shapes to break up a potentially over-strong blocks of color, and 'dilute' the effect with gray, purple or bronze leaves and cream-and-green variegated foliage. This type of bed stands out specially well in a lawn against a background of shrubs. Other combinations include white, silver and mauve, cream, yellow and purple, and mauve, purple and pink.

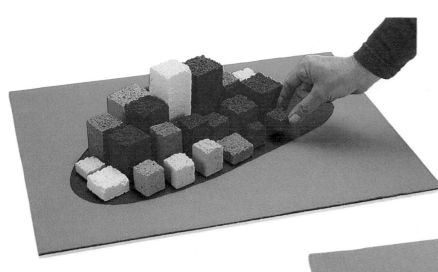

4 Finish off with low spreading or clump-shaped plants around the edge. Try to avoid plants that will spread out over the lawn and make a ragged edge that will look untidy and smother the grass, leaving yellow patches.

5 Rotate the model before finalizing the plan, as it will present a different view from every angle. Plan the 'best' side to face the direction from which you usually see the bed. Remember that one side will be shaded by taller plants in the center and choose varieties accordingly.

Below: *The island bed in the foreground has a red theme, based on Crocosmia 'Lucifer', aided by green and purple foliage and a background of gold and gray.*

Key to plant names

1. Stachys byzantina *'Primrose Heron'*
2. Helenium bigelovii *'Coppelia'*
3. Solidago glomerata *'Golden Thumb'*
4. Crocosmia *'Lucifer'*
5. Kniphofia citrina *'Cobra'*
6. Foeniculum vulgare *'Purpureum'*
7. Hemerocallis *x* luteola *'Mallard'*
8. Kniphofia rufa *'Samuel's Sensation'*
9. Crocosmia *x* crocosmiflora *'Emily McKenzie'*
10. Euphorbia griffithii *'Fireglow'*
11. Phygelius aequalis albus *'Yellow Trumpet'*
12. Penstemon janishiae *'Joy'*
13. Coreopsis verticillata *'Moonbeam'*
14. Imperata cylindrica *'Rubra'*
15. Persicaria milletii
16. Origanum vulgare album *'Aureum'*
17. Imperata cylindrica *'Rubra'*
18. Hemerocallis forrestii *'Frans Hals'*
19. Gaillardia *'Kobold'*
20. Lychnis *x* arkwrightii
21. Achillea *'The Beacon'*
22. Helianthemum *'Ben Heckla'*
23. Phygelius *x* rectus *'African Queen'*
24. Crocosmia *x* crocosmiflora *'Emily McKenzie'*
25. Monarda *'Cambridge Scarlet'*
26. Phlox paniculata *'Prince of Orange'*
27. Hemerocallis *'Stella de Oro'*
28. Hosta fortunei aurea
29. Coreopsis verticillata *'Moonbeam'*

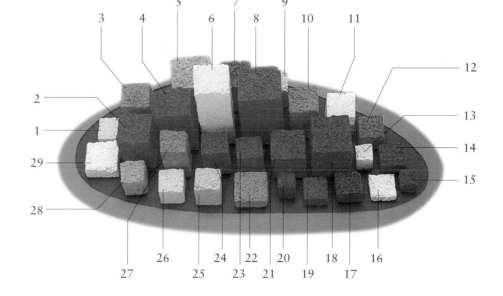

Potted perennials

Perennials make a low-labor alternative to annuals for patio tubs and planters. The same plants can be left in place for three years or more, until they outgrow the space and need dividing. The best subjects are those that are naturally compact and have a long season of interest. Striking foliage plants, such as *Polemonium caeruleum* Brise D'Anjou, *Hakonechloa macra* 'Alboaurea' and *Houttuynia cordata* 'Chameleon', provide color from spring to fall. Hostas are superb for containers, and this is an excellent way to grow them if slugs are a problem in the garden. Simply grease the rim of the pot with petroleum jelly or special crop protection 'glue' to deter the pests. For flowers, choose plants with a long flowering season such as diascia, but use shorter-lived flowers with striking shapes, such as *Agapanthus inapertus* 'Lilliput', for seasonal highlights. Group tubs together so that the foliage of non-flowering kinds enhances whichever flowers are out. For large tubs, choose distinctive specimen plants such as arum lily (*Zantedeschia aethiopica*); this water-lover could be planted in a container without drainage holes and topped up well to keep it wet without continual summer watering.

Right: Sink gardens are a good way to display plants that enjoy hot, well-drained rocky conditions, such as this Diascia rigescens. Unlike many diascias used for annual bedding, this is a hardy perennial species but needs winter protection in cold areas.

Above: Hostas are particular good perennials for containers, but it is important to keep their roots cool and moist, so group several containers together. This is Hosta sieboldiana.

Suitable plants

Agapanthus *(small cultivars e.g. 'Lilliput' and 'Isis')*, Cortaderia pumila *(dwarf pampas grass)*, Hosta, Houttuynia cordata *'Chameleon'*, Imperata cylindrica *'Rubra' and other dwarf grasses, such as Festuca species*, Myosotis scorpioides *'Maytime' (variegated)*, Ophiopogon planiscapus *'Nigrescens'*, Polemonium caeruleum Brise d'Anjou *(striped)*, Zantedeschia aethiopica *'Crowborough' (arum lily)*

All-year schemes

For year-round schemes, choose some of the attractive evergreen perennials. Mix several together in a large container, or grow each kind separately in matching individual pots of different sizes and group them together for an attractive display. Good candidates include Ophiopogon planiscapus 'Nigrescens', *a diminutive lily relative with black linear leaves,* Acorus gramineus 'Ogon', *a grasslike sedge with tufts of narrow green and gold foliage, and* Bergenia beesiana 'Bressingham Ruby', *which has round purple-red leaves. Many of the compact evergreen grasses, such as* Festuca glauca, *make good container plants, too.*

Right: *The new free-flowering dwarf cultivars of agapanthus are specially good patio plants. Agapanthus do not usually start flowering well until they fill the pot with roots, so keep plants well watered to help them establish and avoid repotting until essential.*

Below: *Ornamental grasses do well in pots, but keep them well watered. Festuca species are amongst the most drought tolerant, so choose these if drying may be a problem; they also have the advantage of being evergreen.*

Imperata cylindrica 'Rubra'

Festuca eskia

Festuca 'Blue Glow'

Hakonechloa macra 'Alboaurea'

25

Charming campanulas

The common name 'bellflower' covers a huge range of campanulas, most of which have violet-blue, mauve or white flowers. Plant shapes vary from low, dense, creeping kinds for carpeting rock gardens and growing between cracks in paving, to tall, upright, bushy types for borders. Campanulas have a natural, old-fashioned charm that makes them perfect for a cottage or country-style garden. They tolerate poor or stony soil and wet or dry conditions, and most grow happily in full sun or light shade. However, some kinds tend to be invasive, so choose the right campanula for a given situation. 'Safe' creeping kinds for rock gardens are *C. carpatica* and the delightful 'Elizabeth Oliver', a ground-hugging slow spreader, with a froth of powder-blue, double flowers like baby bells. Save the invasive *C. portenschlagiana* (*C. muralis*) for carpeting areas where its habit of spreading by underground runners is a benefit rather than a nuisance. Place it with care, otherwise the foliage can be swamped by surrounding plants and the plants smothered. *C. glomerata*, the clustered bellflower, has 18in(45cm) stems, topped by clusters of blue flowers in summer; this can be rather invasive and suits a cottage border, shared with others of similar tendencies, or a wildish garden. For a smarter border, choose varieties of *C. lactiflora* and *latifolia*. Both make tall plants about 3-4ft(90-120cm) high, and provide strong stems of bloom in early or midsummer that do not need staking. The most spectacular flowers belong to *C. punctata*, which makes a 12in(30cm)-high, bushy plant covered in summer by long, fat, tubular flowers; the species has off-white spotted flowers; those of the variety 'Rubra' are mauve-pink with a reddish speckled throat. Grow them in front of shrubs at the front of a border. Propagate species campanulas from seed or by division, and named varieties by division in early spring.

Left: Campanula cochleariifolia *is a low-growing plant for the rockery or front of a well-drained border. The small, bell-shaped flowers are held close to the foliage.*

Left: The classic garden campanula, Campanula persicifolia, *has tall spires of open, star-shaped flowers growing above a mat of flat, ground-hugging, leafy rosettes. Blue, mauve and white cultivars are available; all of them associate well with cottage flowers.*

Below: Campanula carpatica *makes neat, compact plants, good for the front of a well-drained border or rockery. They are also grown in pots on cottage windows.*

Cultivation

Perennial campanulas are easy-going plants that grow well in any reasonable soil in sun or partial shade. Mulch around the plants with well-rotted organic matter in early spring. Grow the smaller rockery types in well-drained soil and in a sunny situation or in containers, and topdress the plants with grit or decorative stone chippings.

Above: Campanula latiloba *produces its cup-shaped flowers on 36in(90cm)-tall stems. Most have lavender blue flowers, but the 'Highcliffe Variety' shown here has richer coloring.*

Hot crocosmias

Crocosmia are fabulous flowers for all the bright hot colors; all shades of flaming red, paprika, molten orange and eggyolk yellow are represented. As you might expect, the plants themselves are sunlovers. They like well-drained soil and a sunny spot, tolerating heat and a fair degree of drought once well established. The handsome, broad-grassy foliage grows in neat clumps 24-36in(60-90cm) high, through which wiry stems topped with arching sprays of freesialike blooms appear from midsummer onwards over several months. The trumpet-shaped flowers, arranged in strict order of opening from tight buds at the tip to mature blooms close to the base, form neat triangular sprays that are held immediately above the foliage, which acts as a frame for them. Some cultivars are two-tone; 'Emily MacKenzie', for instance, has orange petals highlighted with red near the center. It also has larger, more wide-open flowers than the traditional type of crocosmia. 'Solfaterre' is another cultivar worth watching for; this has soft apricot flowers and attractive dusky bronze foliage. Crocosmias rarely need splitting up, but when lifted, plants can be propagated by division.

Right: Cultivars with larger-than-usual flowers make a particular impact in a border. This is Crocosmia rosea 'Severn Sunrise', which is a good coppery orange in color.

Below: Crocosmias range in color from pale yellow to bright orange-red; use a mixture of colors throughout a 'hot' border, but do not mix them with pastel shades.

Plant associations

Crocosmias associate well in a bright, sunny border with red hot pokers, hemerocallis, helenium and coreopsis, and are ideal in a red, yellow and orange color scheme. Add grasses, particularly the red Japanese blood grass, for strong contrasts.

Left: *One of the prettiest of the paler crocosmias is 'Solfaterre', an unusual light apricot color almost unique amongst crocosmias and one that would suit a cooler pastel scheme.*

Right: *'Lucifer', as the name suggests, is a devilishly brilliant shade of fiery, luminous red. This popular cultivar is one of the larger-growing kinds, reaching to nearly 48in(120cm) high, given good growing conditions.*

Below: *'Star of the East' has large, wide open flowers almost like miniature lilies, in contrast to the more tubular flowers of many of the better-known crocosmias.*

Improving the soil

On heavy soils, dig in gravel or gritty sand to improve the texture and to raise the height of a bed to improve conditions for crocosmias. They tend to rot if the soil is wet in winter. Alternatively, grow the plants in large containers filled with soil-based potting mix and a little fine grit. Sink the containers to the rim in the soil. You can then lift and store plants under glass from the fall until the following spring.

1 Use gravel, of the type supplied for paths and drives, but ensure that it is washed and free from weedkiller. Spread a 1in(2.5cm) layer over the area to be planted.

2 Mix the gravel well into the soil with a spade or fork before you start to plant. Mix more gravel into the soil that will be used to fill round the roots.

Distinctive daisies

Daisies are essential for a well-furnished border; the characteristic shape of the flowers contrasts strikingly with those of other classic border blooms. Team them with upright spikes, loose sprays and flat-topped heads of achillea for striking effects, or blend them into a mixed perennial border for an informal country-garden look. The Compositae family, to which all daisies belong, is well represented amongst perennial plants, so it is not difficult to find cultivated daisies to suit any situation. They are available in a range of heights, and with flowers in most colors from white through yellow, pink, mauve and purple. The classic daisy has single flowers, with a circle of narrow petals radiating out from a raised central boss, but many cultivated daisies have varieties with double flowers, too. As a general rule, plants in the daisy family are easy to accommodate, being happy in any reasonable garden soil and a fairly sunny situation. The daisy season starts in spring with the yellow doronicum (leopard's bane). In midsummer, coreopsis, echinacea, pyrethrum, rudbeckia, gaillardia, helenium, helianthus and heliopsis provide continuity of daisy flowers throughout the border, followed by perennial asters, such as Michaelmas daisies, in the fall.

Left: Echinacea purpurea *(the coneflower) likes a sunny, well-drained situation. The 36in (90cm)-tall flowers, produced freely all summer, are good for cutting, and attract both bees and butterflies.*

Above: Helenium is commonly known as sneezeweed, as it tends to irritate hay fever sufferers. The flowers are produced throughout late summer; this one is 'Butterpat'.

Above: Coreopsis are short-lived perennials that are good for cutting. The single form shown here is C. grandiflora *'Badengold', while the double form is 'Early Sunrise'.*

Left: Helenium *'Moerheim Beauty' is a popular cultivar in rich autumnal shades. The flowers grow 36in(90cm) high. Like all heleniums, this is an excellent subject for cutting.*

Above: *One of the best perennials is* Rudbeckia fulgida *'Goldsturm'. The plants have a neat, compact habit with flowers produced continuously from early summer until late fall.*

Dividing asters

Perennial asters are easily divided in fall immediately after they finish flowering, or in early spring as new growth starts. The latter is best in cold climates.

Below: *To divide perennial asters, simply dig up a clump and cut it into suitably sized pieces with a sharp spade. Discard old woody material from the middle of the clump and replant healthy divisions from around the edge.*

Michaelmas daisies

Once well-established, most daisies tolerate a certain amount of summer dryness at the roots. In the case of Michaelmas daisies (A. novi-belgii), however, this can make mildew – always a problem with them – even worse; a soil rich in organic matter is helpful, with regular mulches each spring to help moisture retention. Also combat the problem of mildew by changing to other forms of perennial aster, such as New England asters (A. novae-angliae) or A. x frikartii (which flowers a bit earlier, in midsummer) as these are much less susceptible. Aster ericoides cultivars and A. pringlei 'Monte Cassino' are other good alternatives.

Above: *Aster x* frikartii *'Mönch' has a long flowering season – from early midsummer to late fall – and is resistant to mildew.*

Above: *Pyrethrums are floppy plants that have to be supported to stop them smothering their neighbors. They need fertile soil and a sunny situation, and make good cut flowers.*

Right: *Heliopsis, such as this 'Hohlspiegel', are reliable, rugged plants that happily withstand a range of soil conditions. They resemble bushy, perennial sunflowers, and bloom in late summer and fall.*

Euphorbias

Euphorbias are the spurges, a large group of handsome plants with a surprising diversity of character. Their flowers are mainly greenish or yellow, although orange or red appear in some kinds, always arranged in clusters at the tips of the stems. Some euphorbias, such as *E. wulfenii* and *E. mellifera*, are very striking architectural plants and also evergreen. Others, such as *E. dulcis* 'Chameleon' and *E. cyparissius*, are low, bushy and spreading, making good ground cover. These are truly perennial, dying down below ground every winter. There are also some small to medium-sized, low clump or hillock-shaped euphorbias, which are good for raised beds and rock gardens; *E. myrsinites* has overlapping leaves like large glaucous-blue scales running along the sprawling stems, and *E. coralloides* is bushy, with reddish more upright stems. Euphorbias are best known for their ability to withstand hot, dry, impoverished soil and strong sun. However, some kinds also enjoy light shade and richer soil, particularly *E. amygdaloides* and its cultivars (the wood spurges) and *E. griffithii*, some of whose cultivars have striking orange-red stems and bronzy or purplish colored foliage. This makes both kinds good subjects for growing amongst shrubs in mixed borders. One euphorbia, *E. robbiae*, will even live in quite deep shade and makes a useful ground-covering plant for difficult situations, where its slowly creeping underground stems allow it to mingle naturally with other shade-loving plants to create lovely naturalized effects. Perennial euphorbias need no special attention as long as the soil is fairly well drained.

Above: Euphorbia polychroma *blooms in late spring and makes a neat 18in (45cm) dome-shaped plant, ideal for a sunny spot in paving, a rockery or the front of a well-drained border.*

Left: E. characias wulfenii *is a tall, architectural, evergreen plant, topped with huge heads of greeny gold flowers in early summer.*

Growing euphorbia

Plant pot-grown plants in spring or summer; transplant self-sown seedlings in spring while small. Dig up and move established plants of small species in spring; large-growing species, such as E. characias wulfenii *and* E. mellifera *do not transplant well. Choose well-drained soil; sun-loving species tolerate poor dry soil, but need watering until established. Species for light shade, such as* E. amygdaloides, *need richer soil. Add well-rotted compost before planting and mulch annually in spring.*

Below: *For a really hot dry spot, choose* Euphorbia myrsinites. *The stems, clad in overlapping blue-gray scalelike leaves, radiate out in a circle from the root.*

Above: Euphorbia griffithii *'Fireglow' is popular for its fiery red stems and bright orange bracts, It flowers in early summer, grows 36in(90cm) high and enjoys sun or light shade.*

Above: *For more colorful ground cover, allow* Euphorbia dulcis *'Chameleon' to self-seed amongst denser carpeting plants. The purple foliage takes on rich fall tints.*

Pruning euphorbia

Most euphorbias need no pruning; just snip off dead flowerheads and remove old woody stems in the fall. However, E. characias and its subspecies wulfenii do need pruning after flowering to remove the old flowered stems. This makes room for the new shoots that will carry a future crop of flowers, and also removes old stems that will otherwise turn brown and look untidy. However, do this job with great care, as all euphorbias have very irritant sap that often squirts out when plants are damaged.

2 *Plants continue to 'bleed' for some time after cutting; avoid siting euphorbias where stems will get broken by people brushing past. Dispose of prunings carefully.*

1 *When pruning euphorbias, wear gloves and goggles and wash any sap off exposed skin. Wipe secateur blades, as the sap makes them sticky.*

Fabulous ferns

Hardy ferns are the perfect solution for shady areas in the garden where few plants thrive. They do not flower, but more than make up for it with the variety of foliage, which may be lacy, ribbonlike, feathery or ladderlike, depending on species. In general, ferns enjoy good garden soil containing plenty of organic matter to retain moisture; mulching is also beneficial for the same reason. Although ferns are mainly green, there are also silvery and red-tinged kinds. Most hardy ferns die down in winter, but for evergreen foliage, grow the holly fern *(Polystichum* species) which has elegant, triangular, ferny fronds with silvery highlights, and the hart's-tongue fern *(Asplenium scolopendrium)* which makes a vase-shaped plant with deep green, glossy, upright, strap-shaped leaves. Varieties with wavy edges to the leaves, such as *A. s.* 'Crispum Speciosum', are specially attractive. Most ferns have very thin leaves that need humid air and shelter to protect them from drying out and browning; these include the very delicate hardy maidenhair fern *Adiantum venustum* and the bird's foot fern *A. pedatum*, which has maidenhair-like foliage growing from a horseshoe-shaped stem. One of the prettiest of the fragile, thin-leaved ferns is the Japanese painted fern, *Athyrium goeringianum* 'Pictum'; this has wine-red stems and a similar flush to the leaves, which are 'painted' with silver tracings. However, it is slightly tender; in cold regions grow it in a pot and bring it under cover for the winter. For all of these, the protection of a shrub border or light woodland is necessary to provide perfect growing conditions. Few ferns are happy in dry conditions; those that are include the hart's-tongue fern, and some species of *Dryopteris,* including the buckler fern *(Dryopteris filix-mas),* and *Dryopteris affinis* 'Crispa', which has ladderlike leaves.

Right: *Evergreen* Polystichum setiferum *(the soft shield fern) is more tolerant of drier conditions than most ferns, but grows bigger in damper conditions. The foliage makes lacy ladderlike shapes that contrast well with other shade-loving perennials.*

Left: Asplenium scolopendrium *is one of the few evergreen ferns. It succeeds best in light shade in a retentive but well-drained soil and sheltered situation.*

Plant associations

Fern foliage associates wonderfully well with most other shade-tolerant plants that enjoy similar conditions. Team ferns with Solomon's seal, Corydalis flexuosa, *dicentra, hostas, bergenia, pulmonaria, brunnera, hellebores and* Geranium phaeum.

Below: *Team ferns with wild flowers, such as bluebells, and shade lovers, such as hostas, in a wildflower garden or woodland.*

Dryopteris affinis
angustata crispa

Dryopteris filix-
mas 'Crispa
Cristata'

Below: Blechnum spicant *is a useful
evergreen species; it grows in cracks in
walls or on the shady side of a raised
bed or rock garden, and tolerates drier
than average conditions.*

Above: The bird's foot fern, Adiantum
pedatum, *makes a small neat clump
with fanlike leaves made up of dozens
of finely cut leaflets. Here it is shown
growing alongside variegated bamboo.*

Below: Dryopteris ferns are amongst
the best for growing in dryish sites,
although they also thrive in more
traditional damp situations, where
they will grow larger.

Athyrium filix-femina
'Frizelliae'

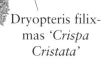

Above: Adiantum venustum, *maidenhair fern, looks good with stonework,
terracotta, fallen logs or by a pool.
Likes moist, humus-rich soil in shade.*

Dryopteris filix-femina
(female fern)

Dryopteris
filix-mas
(male fern)

Versatile geraniums

Do not confuse hardy cranesbills (*Geranium* sp.) with pelargoniums, the frost-tender bedding and pot plants. True geraniums are tough, adaptable, scrambling or mound-shaped plants. They make wonderful flowering ground cover under shrubs and roses all round the garden, and since they are very fashionable, a huge range of both species and named varieties is now available. The color range is mainly blue, mauve and purplish shades, although some geraniums have white, magenta or pink flowers. Old favorites for general ground cover include *G. pratense* 'Mrs Kendall Clarke' and *G. wallichianum* 'Buxton's Variety'. Large, loosely mound-shaped kinds, such as the magenta-flowered *G. psilostemon*, are good towards the front of a border or teamed with other perennial plants. Some sprawling species, such as *G. procurrens*, will scramble up through nearby shrubs. The slightly unusual *G. tuberosum* flowers in early summer, then dies down almost at once, spending summer as dormant tubers underground. It associates well with early perennials, such as pulmonaria, and late spring bulbs. Most geraniums are happy in any good border soil in sun or light dappled shade, but the mourning widow, *G. phaeum*, tolerates more shade than most. The species has flowers so deep purple as to seem black, hence its common name, but named varieties are available with white, lilac and mauve flowers. Small, compact geraniums, such as *G. cinereum*, 'Ballerina' and the delightful low-spreading *G. farreri*, make good plants for a rock garden or the front of a border of treasures such as pinks. They need better-drained soil and fuller sun than the larger more rugged species. Propagate plants by division or basal cuttings taken in spring.

Left: A rare double form of the wild meadow cranesbill, Geranium pratense 'Plenum Violaceum' carries its frilly lavender flowers in midsummer. Grow in sun or shade.

Above: Geranium psilostemon *has vivid magenta flowers with black eyes that appear in early and midsummer. Cut plants back hard after flowering to prevent foliage becoming straggly. New leaves soon appear. Later in the season, plants take on brilliant tints.*

Left: A cultivated form of wild wood cranesbill, 'Bakers Pink', has much softer coloring than the original wild flower. Flowering in early summer, it makes a neat, mound-shaped plant.

Right: Geranium 'Wargrave Pink' is one of the most popular hardy cranesbills; it makes good weed-smothering ground cover in sun or shade, and flowers all summer.

Growing geraniums

Plant pot-grown geraniums in spring or during the summer if they can be kept well-watered in dry spells; lift and divide existing plants in spring. Topdress existing plants each spring with 1in(2.5cm) of sieved garden compost or spent potting mix, tucking it well in amongst the crowns of the plants and over any exposed roots. Geraniums have a habit of lifting themselves up out of the ground as they grow. After a few years, if you do not cover them, you are left with thick stems running along above the soil, with roots virtually hanging in thin air.

Above: Geranium wallichianum *'Buxton's Blue'* is another old favorite, flowering all summer in sun or shade. It self-seeds sparingly, and comes true from seed.

Below: *'Ann Folkard', a hybrid of* G. psilostemon *and* G. procurrens, *has magenta flowers and old-gold leaves. It scrambles pleasingly over the ground and up through shrubs.*

Above: Geranium cinereum *'Ballerina' is ideal for a rock garden or the front of a small border. In sun and well-drained soil, this compact dome-shaped plant flowers all summer.*

Classy grasses

Grasses are incredibly fashionable at present, and with good reason; their dramatic shapes create sparkling contrasts with more colorful flowering plants all season long. Perennial grasses are treated in exactly the same way as herbaceous plants; some do indeed die down in winter, but many are evergreen. These are specially valuable, as their foliage makes wonderful shapes in the winter garden, outlined by frost. The seedheads add elegant architectural shapes and also provide a late feed for birds, both of which add to the enjoyment of the garden long after most flowers are over. With so many kinds to choose from, there are grasses to suit most garden sites and situations. One of the most tolerant – and ideal for poor soil or deep shade under trees – is gardener's garters, *Phalaris arundinacea* 'Picta'. Cultivars of tufted hair grass (*Deschampsia cespitosa*), such as 'Golden Dew', form compact knolls of grassy green foliage from which grow masses of tall, elegant, pale bronze seedheads; this species likes moist soil and light shade. One of the best evergreen grasses is the huge *Stipa gigantea*. The tough all-year-round foliage forms a medium-sized tufted mound, similar in shape to pampas grass. Avoid its sharp-edged leaf blades when weeding. In summer, the center of the tufts erupts into a mass of tall, oatlike stems tipped by nodding seedheads that remain suspended over the plant like a cloud for the rest of the season. Among the smaller ornamental grasses, the most striking is the Japanese blood grass, seen at its best planted where the sun sets behind it, which adds to the impact of the semi-translucent leaves.

Other stunners are *Pennisetum orientale*, which has fat, pinkish, pipecleaner-like flowerheads, and *P. alopecuroides*, which has bottlebrushlike heads. Both are fairly compact and not entirely hardy. Grow them in containers and bring them indoors in winter in cold climates.

Above: Gardener's garters, Phalaris arundinacea *'Picta', has upright green-and-white leaves on plain stems. It can become slightly invasive, but is a useful and decorative 24in (60cm) high grass for ground cover in sun or shade, even on poor, dry soil.*

Below: Ornamental sedges are grouped with grasses as they look similar. Evergreen cultivars, such as Carex elata 'Aurea', (Bowles' golden sedge) make elegant garden plants.

Left: Molinia caerulea *'Variegata' makes an architectural, fountain-shaped plant, whose tall seedheads turn russet brown in the fall.*

Stipa gigantea

Below: *Perennial grasses are available in a huge range of shapes, sizes and textures. Some are grown for their frothy seedheads and others for tall stems or strong foliage.*

Calamagrostis *x* acutiflora *'Karl Foerster'*

Spartina pectinata *'Aureomarginata'*

Miscanthus

Miscanthus are ideal grasses for poor soil, and tolerate wet, heavy clay soils and exposed situations. Most prefer a sunny situation, although a few tolerate some shade. For a windbreak, choose the tall M. sacchariflorus, *which looks a bit like bamboo but does not spread.* M. sinensis *'Zebrinus' and 'Silver Feather' are more decorative tall garden plants, with plumes of flower in late summer and fall. More compact miscanthus cultivars make good feature plants for beds and borders. The stems of miscanthus die in winter and turn brown (some types take on mahogany tints). Cut the old stems down to ground level in early spring, except where plants are grown as a windbreak.*

Above: *In spring, the foliage of* Miscanthus sinensis *'Zebrinus' is green, but the characteristic gold bands appear by midsummer.*

Deschampsia cespitosa

Below: *Plant Japanese blood grass (*Imperata cylindrica *'Rubra') where the sunlight will be behind it; this lights up the leaves, making them look even brighter red than usual.*

Leymus arenarius

Carex buchananii

Carex hachijoensis *'Evergold'*

Festuca glauca

Hellebores

Given the wide range of colors and flower patterns now available among hellebores, it is no wonder that they are so fashionable. The most popular species, *H. orientalis* and *H. niger,* have striking evergreen foliage; many of the less well-known kinds are deciduous, dying down in winter to reappear just before flowering time in spring. Hellebores are easy to grow if conditions are good. Their ideal situation would be woodland clearings, where they get light dappled shade (and certainly protection from strong direct sun), with a free-draining, leafmold-rich soil. In a garden, they grow well amongst shrubs or at the front of a border backed by evergreens, which help to shelter their large, early flowers. Choose a site with well-drained soil rich in organic matter. Improve heavy soil by digging in plenty of grit and bark chippings. Light soil needs plenty of garden compost or well-rotted animal manure to help it hold moisture. Where they are happy, hellebores self-seed and quickly germinate, so that by fall it is usually possible to find tiny seedlings that you can dig up the following spring and pot on singly. They will be ready to plant in the garden after a year. Plants raised from seed take three to four years to flower. Self-sown seedlings left in situ grow faster and often flower slightly sooner. Hellebore plants generally dislike disturbance; if dug up and moved around the garden they can take a year or more to recover.

Left: Helleborus foetidus *has attractive foliage all year, topped in spring by clusters of green flowers; these do not stink, as the name suggests, unless the plant is handled.*

Below: *The blooms of* H. orientalis *range from off-white to various shades of pink. By crossing them with some uncommon hellebores, breeders have introduced a new color range.*

Above: Hellebores are fashionable plants and good new varieties are much in demand. This Helleborus x ericsmithii *takes the name of its hybridizer. Find new varieties in specialist nurseries and by mail order.*

Right: H. nigercors, *a hybrid of* H. niger *and* H. argutifolius *(also called* H. corsicus), *has features of each. The flowers are large, short-stemmed and usually tinged bluish-green. Plants are evergreen and hardy.*

Above: Helleborus niger, *the so-called Christmas rose, rarely flowers so early; mid-spring is the normal time, unless you select special early-flowering forms or grow plants in a greenhouse.*

Left: 'Queen of the Night' *is one of the named varieties of* H. orientalis. *Plants do not come true from seed; named varieties must be propagated vegetatively, which is not easy.*

Right: Helleborus multifidus, *here with rhododendron, is a deciduous species with large, often scented flowers. Team hellebores with other spring and early summer shrubs.*

Hybridizing hellebores

Nurseries hybridize hellebores to produce new named cultivars in a bigger range of colors. Deep pink, misty mauves, hazy purples, plum and nearly black, as well as all shades of green, are always popular. Spotted flowers and those with patterned petals are specially sought after. New cultivars can be expensive to buy, but it is easy to do your own hellebore hybridizing. Since you cannot tell how good a seedling is until it flowers, and it takes three or four years before hellebore seedlings start to flower, you need a reasonable amount of room to grow seedlings to maturity. Once they flower, it is easy to select your favorite colors and patterns. Choose parents with characteristics you want to combine. Select the individual flowers to be crossed carefully. Each hellebore flower contains male parts that bear pollen (anthers, at the tips of the stamens) and female parts that receive the pollen (the stigma, in the center of the flower). When a hellebore flower opens, the stigma matures first and withers before the pollen appears on the anthers; this is a natural mechanism to prevent self-pollination. So to cross-pollinate, you need two flowers at slightly different stages of development. The male parent must have mature anthers and the female parent must have a stigma branching out at the ends, showing that it is receptive to pollen. Leave the female flower on its plant, but pick the male flower to use for pollination.

Crossing solid shades

1 *Choose two plants whose characteristics you want to combine to make the cross. Here a large, deep maroon flower will be the male and a smaller white one the female.*

Crossing to produce a spotted hybrid

The stamens of the 'male' flower

1 *Select a flower with mature anthers to be the 'male' and one with immature anthers and a well developed stigma to be the 'female'.*

The central stigma of the 'female' flower

2 *Dab the male flower into the female to transfer pollen onto the stigma. (Made easier by removing the petals of the male, as shown above.)*

3 *After making the cross, cover the female flower (here) loosely with fleece to stop bees cross-pollinating it. Label the flower with date and name of the cross.*

2 Pick the 'male' flower and remove the petals - this is simply to make it easier to dab its pollen accurately onto the stigma of the 'female' flower.

3 With petals removed, the bristle-like cluster of stamens is like a small brush - use this to gently transfer the pollen onto the tip of the stigma in the center of the 'female'.

The female has small white petals and will 'dilute' the color of the hybrid.

The hybrid has pale maroon flowers slightly smaller than the original 'male'.

The male of this cross has large, deep maroon flowers.

4 The seedpods develop inside the fleece and the ripe seeds will be trapped ready for collection. Sow them immediately - the seeds do not germinate well unless sown fresh.

The 'male' flower has pink petals heavily marked in maroon.

The 'female' flower has white petals with just a few spots.

The resulting hybrid has white petals with a bold patterning of maroon spots.

Hemerocallis

Hemerocallis are the day lilies, so-called because each large, trumpet-shaped flower only lasts for a day. However, each 24-36in(60-90cm)-high flower spike produces a succession of blooms that open a few at a time to provide a long sequence of opening, and each plant has a number of spikes in production at any one time, with more in the offing. In this way, day lilies continue flowering for about two months; timing varies slightly according to variety, but midsummer is the main day lily flowering season. The plants themselves form fountainlike shapes of gracefully arching, strap-shaped foliage about 24in(60cm) tall. They are very hardy and easy to grow, preferring a sunny spot although they tolerate a little light shade. Flower colors are hot; chiefly yellows, tawny orange and buffs, although many of the latest new varieties are stunning shades of red, mahogany and maroon. A few pink shades are also sometimes available.

Above: Hemerocallis flowers have an elegant, classic shape, very similar to that of bulbous lilies. Use them to add brilliance to borders or in amongst shrubs. This is H. lilioasphodelus (H. flava), which grows to 39in(1m).

Plant associations

Day lilies make striking feature plants for pride of place in a sunny perennial border, while clumps planted among the shrubs in a mixed border add seasonal effect. Team them with tall grasses, such as Stipa gigantea or miscanthus, or among perennials with strong upright shapes, such as lupins, for a striking plant association. Use bright hemerocallis with other red, orange and yellow flowers in contrasting shapes, such as helenium, red hot poker and phygelius, to create a striking hot sunny border, and at the same time extend the flowering season of the whole group. Use individual plants or small groups as a feature in a lawn or next to a path.

Left: 'Superlative' is an exciting shade of mahogany red; this distinctive flower color associates beautifully with both pink and orange flowers in a border; use it to tone down a bed of hot colors.

Right: In time, hemerocallis builds up into large, shapely clumps. There is no need to divide them until the plants start to flower sparsely; then lift, split and replant in spring. This is Hemerocallis 'Norton Orange'.

Plant care

Hemerocallis enjoy a rich soil, so mulch them annually in spring with rich, well-rotted garden compost or manure and feed them with a high-potash fertilizer to promote vigorous blooming. In time, plants make large clumps that can be quite difficult to dig up and divide. In this case, it is permissable to simply slice through the plant and dig out half, making room for fresh, young, free-flowering shoots.

Left: Tawny orange is the color traditionally associated with hemerocallis. This 'Prima Donna' has particularly attractive streaked flowers with lightly crimped edges.

Right: 'Summer Wine' is a remarkable pinky-mauve shade, which can be quite difficult to place in the garden, but associates especially well with pink, maroon and lavender shades.

Below: Bicolored day lily flowers are particularly striking; the individual blooms can almost resemble those of gladioli. This cultivar is an unusual one, 'Mrs David Hall'.

Above: 'Millie Schlumpf' is an unusual color rarely seen in hemerocallis; use pale pink cultivars in pastel schemes or to brighten foliage gardens. This one will grow to about 20in(50cm).

Fashionable hostas

For many gardeners, hostas, commonly known as plantain lilies, are the first choice when it comes to picking plants for a moist, shady spot. However, they are also happy in sun, provided the soil remains damp, and in shade the plants tolerate drier soil than is often believed. Hostas are slow-growing, small to medium-sized, clump-forming plants with pronounced ribs. Although they do flower, the spikes of off-white or pale mauve bell- or trumpet-shaped flowers are not very striking except in a few isolated varieties, and plants are mainly grown for their outstandingly attractive foliage. There are two basic types of plants: those with medium-sized, thin, oval to heart-shaped foliage, which may be strongly variegated, gold or green, such as *H. fortunei* 'Picta' and the curly leaved *H. undulata* 'Medio-Variegata'; and those with fewer, but larger and thicker, puckered, paddle-shaped leaves that are often a glaucous blue color, such as *H. sieboldiana* 'Elegans' and 'Frances Williams'. Hostas are immensely collectable. Expect to pay high prices for the latest new varieties that are constantly coming out, although old favorites are cheaper. The reason is that plants have to be propagated by division, and it takes several years before clumps are large enough to be split up. New plants are also slow to establish, so propagation is a long, slow process and nurseries are invariably unable to produce as many hostas as they could sell.

Above: Hosta undulata *makes dense clumps of small wavy-edged leaves. The plants are very slow-growing and rarely need dividing.*

Right: Gold and variegated-leaved hostas are a great way to brighten up a shady spot; add plenty of well-rotted compost to the soil to help it retain moisture. Here are 'Frances Williams' (back), 'Wide Brim' (left) and 'Gold Standard' (right), all large-leaved cultivars.

Slug damage

All hosta foliage is notoriously attractive to slugs and snails, which can quickly reduce leaves to holes or even bare skeltons, with only ribs remaining. Protecting plants from attack is one of the main worries of hosta growers, and a variety of techniques can be used, including slug pellets, old-fashioned beer traps, and growing plants near a pond, so that frogs, etc., can control the pests naturally.

Typical slug damage on a hosta leaf.

Plant associations

Combine hostas with plants whose flower spikes provide a sharp contrast to the hosta leaves. Blue-leaved hostas look good with pink, orange or yellow flowers. Team variegated hostas with yellow, mauve or white flowers. In damp soil, grow hostas with candelabra primulas, astilbe and mimulus. In shade, combine them with contrasting leaf shapes of ivy, hardy ferns and flowers of foxglove and Alchemilla mollis. In a sunnier spot or dappled shade, use persicaria, hardy cranesbill or ornamental grasses.

Above: Hostas that not only have good foliage but also pretty flowers are quite hard to find; most hostas have unspectacular white flowers. This attractive specimen is 'Blue Secret'. Its flowers last well in shade.

Right: 'Sun Power' has pale gold foliage that teams well with variegated hostas and Alchemilla mollis. The leaf color of gold hostas is brightest in light shade; in heavy shade it turns greenish and in sun it bleaches.

Left: The leaves of H. sieboldii are strikingly textured with light green ribs and 'dimples' – one reason why this and other hostas make such valuable additions to foliage gardens in shady situations. They associate well with grasses such as Hakonechloa.

Look for shoots at this stage when dividing hostas

Dividing hostas

1 *Hostas do not need dividing until an old crown looks congested or dies out in the middle, say every five years or so. Divided plants take a year or more to establish, so do not be surprised if they do not make much new growth to start with.*

You can propagate a hosta either as soon as you buy a new plant or after it has been growing in a pot or in the garden for some time. When buying a new hosta, choose a pot-grown plant with as many shoots as possible. In spring, divide it into two or more pieces, depending on the number of shoots, and repot each piece separately; they will be too small to plant out in the garden at this stage. Use a cold frame in a shady spot as a nursery, and plunge the pots into a deep bed of peat litter or rich soil so they cannot dry out. Protect from slugs and snails, keep well watered and feed the plants regularly with a general-purpose liquid feed. They should be big enough to plant out in the garden after a year or two. Existing hostas are probably best left undisturbed until they actually need dividing, as plants can be slow to re-establish. Leave those in the garden until the clump outgrows its space, or plants lack vigor or the center of an old clump starts to die out. Lift and divide established hostas in early spring, ideally before the leaves start unfurling. If they are divided when the leaves are fully open, they will lose a great deal of water before the new roots have developed.

2 *This pot-grown hosta has filled its pot with roots and there is little room for new growth to emerge. Divide it in spring when the first shoots are just visible.*

3 *Look to see which shoots form small natural groups. Use a strong, sharp knife to cut and lever apart the rootball, dividing the plant into small clumps as you work.*

4 *A hosta such as this, planted in a 15in(38cm) pot, makes about five good-sized divisions. Do not be tempted to make several very small plants, as these will take a long time to develop into good new specimens.*

5 *Repot each division into a pot that is 1in(2.5cm) bigger all round than the rootball. Use good-quality potting mixture, not garden soil.*

6 Add more potting mix, trickling it down between the shoots so each part of the plant can root easily. Tap the pot gently down to settle the mix.

7 Gently firm the mix around the roots. Leave a gap of about 0.5in (1.25cm) below than the rim of the pot to allow for watering later on.

Planting a young hosta in the garden

Plant young hostas out in spring the year after propagating them. Prepare the soil in the planting area by digging in plenty of well-rotted organic matter, such as garden compost. Hostas often fail to establish because the plants are grown in peat-based mixes in their pots by nurseries and then planted into garden soil with low levels of organic matter. This means that the roots never spread out from the original rootball into the surrounding soil.

Below: Plant new hostas at the same level as they were growing previously. When moving plants from elsewhere in the garden, look for the soil mark on the young stems as a guide.

8 Water until all the mix is evenly moist. Allow the surplus to drain away through the holes in the bottom of the pot; do not stand it in a saucer. Keep slightly dry for a few weeks while new roots form.

Smaller divisions are best grown on in pots for a year. If after that they are still very small, move them to a size larger pot and fresh potting mix and wait a further year.

9 If dividing a large clump of hostas dug up from the garden, make each division 4-6in (10-15cm) across. These are big enough to replant straight back into the garden after improving the soil with organic matter and general fertilizer.

Classic irises

The iris family includes water and bog garden plants, bulbs and rock garden plants, but the best known members are the bearded irises, which are classic border perennials. All irises have a unique flower shape that makes them easily recognizable anywhere. This is made up of three upward-curving petals called 'standards' and three downward-curving petals called 'falls'. In the case of bearded iris, each of the three falls also has a tuft of hair along its midline – the 'beard' from which the type gets its name. Bearded iris grow from thick tubers (technically called rhizomes) that lie half-buried in the soil; from these grow the sword-shaped evergreen leaves and flower spikes that appear on tall stems in early midsummer. As the clump expands, the tubers of bearded iris branch and spread outwards, and the oldest sections in the center of the clump die away, leaving the plant with a hollow center. After three to five years, depending on growth rate, bearded iris therefore need to be dug up and divided.

Do this in midsummer about six weeks after flowering finishes. Plant young tubers, or new plants of bearded iris, in well-drained soil, leaving the top surface of the tubers exposed to light in a very sunny situation without any risk of shade. If planted too deep, or where other plants shade the tubers, bearded iris will not flower.

Right: 'Jane Phillips' is a very fine blue cultivar, with clear, almost violet-blue flowers with ruffled petals; the flower spikes stand 36in(90cm) high.

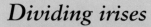

1 *Divide clumps of iris with a knife. Each piece must contain at least one mature section of rhizome, plus one or more 'pups'.*

2 *Each division also needs a reasonable root system. Discard any with gnarled, leafless rhizomes, as they will not flower well.*

3 *Trim the foliage in an inverted V shape 2-3in(5-7.5cm) from the base. This reduces water loss, so the new plant can establish well.*

4 *If replanting the new division in the original site, first improve the soil with general fertilizer and some well-rotted organic matter.*

5 *Replant young sections of tuber horizontally, with the top of the rhizome above the ground, but the base in the soil. The new roots will develop from this part of the plant. Firm gently after planting and water in thoroughly.*

Left: Blues and yellows are the traditional bearded iris colors, although nowadays a huge range is available, some with very attractively marked or ruffled flowers.

Range of plants

Bearded irises are available in unusual mahogany, gold and brownish shades, as well as all the popular pastels and blues. Many varieties have attractive two-tone flowers, with the standards and falls in contrasting colors. Some varieties (usually from specialist nurseries) have truly enormous flowers, and these need more sheltered situations to protect the blooms.

Above: The combination of lilac standards and purple falls with ruffled petals make some iris cultivars resemble the flowers of an exotic cattleya orchid.

Above: The two-tone appearance of 'Black Douglas' flowers are made up of purple standards (the upward-turning petals) and indigo-black falls (the petals that curve downwards).

Right: Bronze-orange shades are some of the most sensational to be found in bearded irises. The darker veining on this cultivar, 'Action Front', is a particularly attractive feature.

Stylish lilies

Although they are strictly bulbs, lilies are well-qualified for inclusion as honorary perennials. They are traditional inhabitants of a herbaceous border, remaining in place for many years until clumps need dividing, and dying down each winter. Lilies like a situation that allows their stems to grow in sun, while their roots are in cool shade cast by surrounding plants. They are exceptionally heavy feeders and need deep, rich soil with plenty of organic matter. Bulbs will rot in heavy soil that lies wet in winter. Apply thick mulches of well-rotted manure or other rich material each spring. Additional liquid feeding with tomato feed during the season, plus watering to prevent dryness at the roots during the growing season, are also beneficial. The classic lily of cottage gardens is the Madonna lily *(Lilium candidum)*. Plant it shallowly, so that the very tip of each bulb is just visible above the surface of the soil. *Lilium regale,* another country garden classic, has strongly scented white flowers. If scent is a priority, choose named varieties from a group of lilies known as oriental hybrids; although equally colorful, many other hybrids are unscented.

Most lilies need lime-free soil, although it need not be particularly acid. If the garden soil is unsuitable for lilies, either due to winter wet or the presence of chalk, grow the plants in large pots of ericaceous potting mix, plunged to the rim in borders each spring. Store the bulbs, still in their pots, in a cold or barely frost-free green-house or sunroom for the winter.

Above: Lilium regale, *a species lily, grows well in both heavy and light soil, with or without lime, and in sun or light shade. The large midsummer blooms make good cut flowers; the stems can reach more than 39in(1m). Mulch with well-rotted compost and apply a general fertilizer in spring.*

Planting lilies

Plant new lilies in fall or spring, depending on the availability of the bulbs. Plant deeply – about three times the depth of the bulb. Do not allow bulbs to dry out before planting or when moving dormant bulbs to another part of the garden, which can also be done in spring or fall. Plant in rich, well-drained but moisture-retentive soil.

1 *Fork plenty of well-rotted manure into the base of the planting hole and soil. Sit the bulb in the hole and press in gently.*

2 *Plant groups of three or five bulbs about 12-18in(30-45cm) apart and cover them with three times their own depth of soil.*

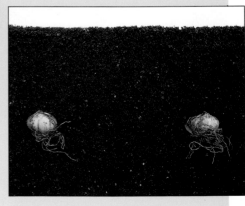

Above: *The scented flowers of Lilium longiflorum are favorites for floristry; the plants are not hardy; grow them in pots on the patio in summer or keep them in a sunroom.*

Propagating tiger lily bulbils

1 *You can propagate the tiger lily,* Lilium tigrinum, *using bulbils that form in the leaf axils where the leaves join the stem.*

2 *After the flowers are over, in late summer and early fall, pick off the bulbils when they are about pea-sized or slightly bigger.*

3 *Press the bulbils gently into a pot of seed mixture, leaving the tips of each bulbil just showing. You can plant several in one pot.*

4 *Water with a fine rose to settle the bulbils into the mix. They root rapidly and the young plants will flower in their second year.*

Lily pollen stains, so snip the anthers from lilies used for cutting.

Left: *Compact lily cultivars are often sold by garden centers as potplants for house or garden use; plant the bulbs in the garden after the flowers are over.*

Left: *Lilies hybridize readily and you can grow some very interesting plants just by sowing the seeds that form on plants in the garden in late summer. They usually take about three years to flower. This is a pink hybrid of* Lilium regale.

53

Brilliant poppies

Oriental poppies herald the start of the summer herbaceous border season. They are one of the first classic perennials to flower, producing huge cabbagey heads of brightly colored but fragile-looking crumpled petals surrounding a central 'pepper-pot' seed capsule. Named varieties offer flowers in the traditional ladybird red, gleaming white or salmon pink. The petals of many cultivars have black bases that give a contrasting dark center to the flowers. Individual blooms only last a few days and the total flowering season is limited to just a few weeks. However, after the petals drop, the seed capsules left at the ends of the bare flower stems provide a decorative feature in their own right, as does the jagged, bristly, almost thistlelike foliage. This persists for most of the summer, but can become untidy; if left alone it dies down early, leaving a terrible gap in the border. This can be masked by planting late-flowering perennials around the poppies. Alternatively, cut back all the foliage and old flower stems virtually to ground level soon after flowering is finished. The plants respond by producing a second crop of fresher foliage that lasts the season, acting as a foliar foil to the flowers of surrounding plants. Oriental poppies need a sunny spot and do best in rather poor soil; excess nutrients can encourage leafy growth at the expense of good flowering. Well-drained soil is vital for winter survival; on wet, heavy soil the thick fleshy roots rot easily.

Left: Oriental poppies have huge flowers with fragile, crumpled petals that last little more than a day before dropping; each plant produces new flowers regularly over several weeks.

Popular cultivars

'Black and White': white petals with black central blotch
'Ladybird': vermilion red
'Mrs Perry': salmon pink
'Curlilocks': orange-red petals with heavily ruffled edges
'Perry's White': outstanding shining gray-white
'Goliath': huge red flowers

Right: Oriental poppies make good plants for growing in isolation or with a foliage plant for 'back-up'. This one is teamed with a dryopteris fern, one of the few kinds suitable for a dryish soil and open situation.

Below: 'Mrs Marrow's Plum', also known as 'Patty's Plum', is an unusual oriental poppy cultivar, with mauve coloring and black blotches near the base of the pleated petals.

Right: *Although most oriental poppies have flowers of one color, a few bicolored kinds are occasionally available. This cultivar is called 'Pinnacle'.*

Left: *Some of the pink poppies are particularly beautiful; this one is called 'Helen Elisabeth'. The petals are most strongly crinkled when the flowers first open.*

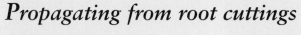

Propagating from root cuttings

Oriental poppies can be dug up and divided in fall or early spring when clumps are too big or need rejuvenating. However, if you need a number of plants of the same variety, the best way to propagate them is from root cuttings. Dig up an established plant in late summer or early fall and remove one or two entire roots from the base of the plant. Cut the thickest part into 3-4in(7.5-10cm) lengths and, keeping the pieces the right way up, push them vertically into pots of sandy seed mix so that the top of the cutting is level with the surface of the mix. Keep the cuttings in a greenhouse and water sparingly until the young plants are big enough to pot on separately.

Diverse primulas

Primulas are spring- and early summer-flowering plants that add bright splashes of color to borders and watersides. Their flowers grow on stems of varying lengths originating from a large, loose rosette of long oval leaves. The best-known primulas are the small drumstick primula (*Primula denticulata*) and colored forms of common primrose (*P. vulgaris*), which flower in early spring. Gold-laced polyanthus resemble primroses with blackish flowers, whose petals are thinly edged with a band of gold. Once scarce, these choice plants are now becoming much more widely available. They are perfectly hardy and grow well in similar conditions to primroses; provide moist soil with plenty of humus and light shade.

The spectacular candelabra primulas have flowers arranged in tiers, rather like floral wedding cakes. Several different species fall into this category, such as *P. japonica* and *P. pulverulenta*. These stunning plants enjoy damp soil in a fairly sunny spot, and are often grown around ponds, where their reflections double the display. The giant Himalayan cowslip (*P. florindae*) needs the same conditions; it has a large ball of loosely packed nodding yellow blooms on each flower spike. All three grow to about 30in(75cm) high. *Primula vialii* has upright spikes of mauve flowers and thrives in light shade in a border with shrubs or other moisture-loving perennials.

Left: The charming wild primrose (Primula vulgaris) thrives in damp to wet soil, including heavy clays, and in shade. It is useful for wild corners where many plants will not grow.

Below: Old varieties of double primrose, such as this 'Marie Crousse', are much weaker growing than modern ones. Divide plants every three years to rejuvenate them. Grow in rich soil in a moist shady spot.

Below: The flowers of Primula vialii are like 12in(30cm)-high pokers in mauve tipped with red. Plants need light, dappled shade and rich, moist soil with plenty of organic matter.

Right: One of the candelabra primulas, Primula bulleyana *is ideal for bog garden conditions. Plants grow 2-3ft(60-90cm) tall and have large oval leaves. Where happy, they will self-seed, so watch out for seedlings when weeding around the plants.*

Below: Primula alpicola *grows 18in (45cm) tall, with nodding bunches of fragrant cowsliplike flowers. Grow in light shade and a soil rich in humus. It is known as the moonlight primula because of the pale yellow flowers.*

Propagating primulas

Primulas are often rather short-lived and need refreshing periodically. To grow new plants of named varieties divide up old plants; do this in early spring, so that each division has three or four crowns; replant into improved soil and water well until established. Good-sized divisions should flower the same year. Species and named seed strains are easily grown from seed. Sow bought seed in spring on the surface of moist seed mix in a shady spot in a greenhouse or at a cool window indoors. Where happy, primula plants in the garden will shed seed; the seedlings are hybrids, but they provide some very good plants for free. Dig them up and pot them on, or allow them to grow where they appear naturally.

Right: Primula denticulata, *the drumstick primula, appears in early spring, so needs protection from hard frosts. Flowers appear from a rosette of partially developed foliage and may be white, mauve or lilac.*

Perennials for scent

Flowers:

Cosmos atrosanguineus *(dark chocolate)*, Crambe cordifolia *(honey)*, Dianthus, Euphorbia mellifera *(honey)*, Hemerocallis 'Catherine Woodbery' and 'Cream Drop' Hosta 'Honeybells', Iris graminea *(plum tart)* Phlox

Foliage:

Agastache foeniculum, Aloysia triphylla *(lemon)*, Anthemis cupanina *(chamomile)*, Geranium macrorrhizum, *Mint*, Monarda *(lemon)*, Nepeta, Salvia officinalis *(sage)*

Flowers and foliage:

Dictamnus albus *(lemon)*

Above: Hemerocallis 'Catherine Woodbery' *has an attractive lilylike perfume. The pink flowers (unusual for a hemerocallis) team well with pastel shades in a scented border.*

Below: Phlox paniculata *has a sweet spicy perfume. The pink and white varieties seem more strongly scented. They bring welcome fragrance to late summer gardens.*

Perfumed perennials

Many perennial plants are deliciously scented, which adds to the beauty of their flowers and foliage. For best effect, dot perfumed plants around the garden, so that each individual fragrance stands alone. When too close together, strong scents, such as lavender, overwhelm subtler ones, such as the plum tart iris *(Iris graminea)* and chocolate cosmos *(Cosmos atrosanguineus)*, and when several pronounced perfumes mingle, the effect can be overpowering rather than attractive. The scent of some plants comes from the flowers, so their season of scent can be a short one. Quite surprising flowers often prove to have delicate scents when investigated at close quarters; try some cultivars of hemerocallis and hosta. With other plants, it is the foliage that is scented. The leaves contain essential oils that are only released into the air when they are gently bruised. Plants with scented leaves have a much longer scent 'season', but need planting where people will brush past them – at the side of a path or even in cracks between paving. Grow scented plants of all sorts next to doorways, windows that are left open in summer, on the patio and beside garden seats to make the most of them; some are highly suitable for container cultivation.

Plant perfumes linger best on still, humid air, so a warm sheltered situation is preferable. High temperatures and dryish soil tend to concentrate scent, and fragrance is often stronger in the evening.

Right: *The Himalayan cowslip* (Primula florindae) *has the most powerful perfume of any of the primulas, and flowers a little later than most species, in midsummer.*

58

Left: Geranium macrorrhizum *flowers in late spring, but it is the foliage that is scented. The faint rose scent is released whenever the leaves are bruised, so position the plant by a garden path.*

Right: When crushed, the ferny foliage of Chamaemelum nobile *releases a fresh 'green apple' scent. Plant it by a sunny path where creeping sprigs will be trodden on to release its fragrance.*

Releasing scents

A few plants need processing to produce their scent; Iris 'Florentina' has mildly perfumed flowers, but when grated, dried and powdered, the roots are orrisroot – used as a fixative for potpourri – which is scented of violets. Cut and dried, sweet woodruff (Asperula odorata) has a fragrance like new-mown hay. Use the foliage of scented plants such as bergamot in potpourri. Bergamot leaves also flavor tea.

Below: Scented-leaved plants, such as this catmint Nepeta x faasenii, *make good plants to grow around garden seats, where their perfume helps to create a relaxing environment.*

Cosmos atrosanguineus

The flowers have a subtle aroma of dark chocolate. Avoid planting it near other scented plants; the smell 'fights' with flowery fragrances.

Above: When deadheading, cut the stem back to its point of origin with a leafy stem. Do not confuse unopened buds with dead heads.

Left: The flowers of chocolate-scented cosmos look best when seen against the sunlight, which makes them brighter. Individual flowers only last a few days.

Unopened bud

Open flower

Remove dead heads often to keep plants flowering.

59

An heirloom border

If you like gardening tempered with a measure of nostalgia, then heirloom plants are for you. Plants from the past have an old-fashioned charm, and are often scarce collectables, treasured by enthusiasts. Since many heirloom plants are small species, and weak or slow growers, it makes sense to group them in a sheltered situation with well-drained soil, where you can give them extra care and save them from being swamped by more robust neighbors. Most enjoy soil containing plenty of well-rotted organic matter. Avoid overfeeding, as this can make plants grow out of character; the resulting soft growth is often prone to problems. Heirloom perennials can be idiosyncratic, but to enthusiasts this is all part of their attraction. Old pinks have a short flowering season in early midsummer that coincides with that of old roses. Many varieties are heavily scented of cloves or spices, and some varieties were once grown in tavern gardens where the flowers were used in mulled ale. They need a very sunny spot, with light, well-drained soil and no organic matter. Plants are shortlived, so propagate from cuttings in summer every three years. Double wallflowers, such as 'Harpur Crewe' and 'Bloody Warrior', bloom in late spring and early summer and enjoy some protection from strong midsummer sun and plenty of organic matter in well-drained soil. Propagate from cuttings every two to three years; being double-flowered, they do not produce seed.

Old varieties of cultivated primrose are charming for a cool spot in light shade with rich organic soil. 'Garryarde Guinevere' has mauve leaves and pink flowers; 'Jack in the Green' primroses have large green calyxes. Specially delightful are the many Victorian varieties of violets, including the strongly perfumed Parma violets that need cold frame protection in winter. Old violets and violas all need rich, well-drained soil and partial shade; they are ideal for growing in pots.

Below: Antique violas often have colors or patterns not seen in modern hybrids. This attractive Viola *'Jackanapes' takes the name of Gertrude Jekyll's pet monkey.*

Right: Dianthus *'Inchmery' is an 18th century pink, known for its outstanding perfume. The well-behaved flowers open fully without the calyx splitting, a common fault with many of the old double pinks. The pink flowers contrast well with the silvery foliage.*

Above: Dianthus *'Nancy Lindsay' is a heavily scented old single pink, treasured by Nancy Lindsay and rescued from her garden after her death. It makes a compact plant, but like all old pinks, it is shortlived and needs replacing often. Take cuttings every two to three years.*

Auricula theaters

Show auriculas (special cultivars of Primula auricula with a powdery covering to the foliage and large flowers, often with green or gray centers) were traditionally displayed in special 'theaters' while in flower. These were tiers of narrow shelves, backed by black velvet to give the plants a dramatic background; very few still exist. Nowadays, however, rows of shelving with an all-weather backdrop make a nice way to display any choice, compact, collectors' plants flowering in pots.

Below: *Of the hundreds of named varieties that once existed, we now only have gold-laced and silver-laced polyanthus. Best grown in the ground in similar conditions to primroses and divided every two to three years.*

Right: *'Hose in Hose' primroses look as if they have two-tier flowers with one growing from the center of another. When several old primroses and gold-laced polyanthus are grown close together, they will cross-pollinate. The resulting self-sown seedlings are new hybrids, often with very striking flowers. They are not the original varieties, but are worth keeping.*

Right: *Old double primroses, such as this 'Quaker's Bonnet', are popular with collectors. Plants need well-drained but humus-rich soil in light shade. Divide them every few years in mid- to late summer.*

Perennials to treasure

Collecting rare plants or the latest new varieties is a great hobby with some perennial gardeners. Hunting hard-to-get 'treasures' at remote nurseries and plant fairs is all part of the fun. You can get to know fellow enthusiasts at meetings of specialist societies and swapping cuttings is a good way to obtain scarce plants. Many societies organize seed distribution schemes for members, hold conferences or arrange plant-oriented holidays and outings. Plants such as hostas and hemerocallis are traditionally popular with collectors. Find new varieties by putting your name on the mailing lists of good nurseries, or read about them in specialist journals. Some of the best 'new' introductions of recent years include the variegated *Polemonium* Brise D'Anjou, several named varieties of *Corydalis flexuosa* (a blue-flowered spring woodlander that dies down each summer) and *Phlox divaricata* 'Blue Dreams', which has scented light blue flowers. Some plants remain rare because they are slow or difficult to propagate; many have interesting stories that make them novel conversation pieces for the garden. Grow rare or new plants that are hard to replace in pots plunged to their rims in a sand-bed and give them extra care until they are big enough to propagate from. To give the offspring the best chance of survival, plant them in several places in the garden where they will not be swamped by vigorous neighbors. Always give a few young plants away to like-minded friends; that way you can be sure of getting a replacement if your own are lost.

Above: Anthemis *'Susanna Mitchell'* is a superb new cultivar that produces a succession of large flowers throughout the summer. Grow in full sun on well-drained, even poor soil. Ideal for banks or borders with hot, dry, infertile soil.

Below: Mosquito grass (Bouteloua gracilis) *has curious flowerheads held at right angles to the stem. Plants grow 12in(30cm) tall and need light, well-drained soil and a sheltered sunny spot where the fragile stems will not get broken.*

Left: Ranunculus ficaria *'Flore Pleno' is a double-flowered form of the wild celandine. The many named varieties vary slightly in their flower shapes. In a spot with moist, heavy soil and light dappled shade, cultivated celandines spread slowly.*

Left: Corydalis flexuosa *is a choice spring-flowering plant for light dappled shade and well-drained soil rich in humus. Plants die down earlier than most perennials, but this is normal; do not imagine that they are dead. Mark the spot where they are planted so that they are not uprooted.*

Left: An improved form of gardeners' garters, Phalaris arundinacea 'Feesey', has green-and-white striped foliage that looks mostly white from a distance. This form spreads less vigorously than the original and is good for brightening dull spots under trees. It prefers moist, humus-rich soil in sun or shade.

Left: The pale blue flowers of Polemonium *Brise D'Anjou are not very showy, so where the plant is wanted for foliage, remove the flower stems as soon as they appear so the plant puts all its energy into growing more and better variegated foliage.*

Above: The normal mountain cornflower (Centaurea montana) has plain green leaves, but this cultivar 'Gold Bullion' is a most attractive variation. It flowers in early and midsummer. If cut back straight after, a second flush of flowers may appear.

Perennials for cutting

Above: *To save cutting flowers you do not eventually use, take a vase into the garden and see how it looks with your flowers. You will also get a good idea of how many stems you need and what length to cut them.*

Many perennial plants, including scabious, pinks, gypsophila and hosta, provide good flowers and foliage for cutting. In most cases, you can remove a few flowers during the season without spoiling the look of the border. Cut stems from the back of the plant or 'thin out' the center of a large clump so that any gaps are less noticeable. To avoid wastage, look carefully at the flowers before cutting and reject any that may prove unsuitable due to insect pests, weather damage, short stems, etc. Pick only perfect blooms; slight imperfections are less noticeable on flowers in the garden. When cutting flowers, take a bucket of tepid water into the garden and stand the stems in deep water immediately after cutting. If flowers are unavoidably left out of water for any time, cut 1in(2.5cm) or more from the base of the stems using a sharp knife to make a long sloping cut. (This increases the area through which the stems can take up water.) Leave the flowers standing in water up to their necks overnight before arranging them.

Fresh flowers

To keep cut flowers fresh, avoid bacteria building up in the water and blocking the stems. Rinse vases in diluted bleach between uses and change the water regularly. Commercial cut-flower feeds, available from florists, provide nutrients, and some brands contain antibacterial agents to keep the water clean without changing it. Some people use fizzy lemonade or add sugar or an aspirin to the water to help flowers last longer.

Above: *The flowers of Astrantia major, known as Hattie's pincushion, are good for cutting. Despite their appearance, they do not dry well.*

Left: *With their metallic tints and spiky heads, sea hollies, either fresh or dried, make great plants for flower arrangers. This is Eryngium planum 'Silver Ghost'. Grow eryngiums in very well-drained soil in full sun.*

Above: *You do not need to be an experienced flower arranger to get good results; a simple bunch of daisies sitting loosely in a plain jar makes a pleasing country-style display that brings the garden indoors.*

Suitable plants

Aster *'Monte Cassino'*, Astilbe, Bergenia *flowers and foliage*, Centaurea macrocephala, Chrysanthemum rubellum *vars.*, Crocosmia, Delphinium, Dianthus, Dicentra, Echinops ritro, Eryngium, Gypsophila paniculata, Helenium, Helianthus, Hosta *foliage*, Lythrum salicaria, Paeonia, Persicaria, Phlox, Phygelius, Platycodon, Scabiosa, Sedum spectabile, Sidalcea, Solidago, Veronica gentianoides, Zantedeschia

Right: Dedicated arranger-gardeners often like to use gardening equipment as containers for arrangements of border flowers. Nowadays, all kinds of attractively colored and even hand-painted cans and pots are available.

Below: Brightly colored, distinctively shaped flowers are always popular with arrangers; this is Crocosmia 'Vulcan'. Cut the stems when the first few flowers at the base of the spike are just open. This way, the blooms will last a long time in water.

A 'cutting bed'

Serious flower arrangers find that a special 'cutting bed' provides them with plenty of material without ruining their borders. Grow suitable plants in rows, nursery style, keep them well fed and watered for peak productivity and stake them to ensure straight stems. Use a good mixture of plants to supply flowers of various shapes and sizes all season long, and include plenty of foliage plants.

Below: As soon as you have cut the flowers, place the stems into a deep bucket of tepid water. This prevents air being drawn into the end of the stems and helps flowers last longer.

Perennials to attract butterflies and bees

A wide variety of birds, butterflies and bees are attracted into gardens by perennials that provide nectar, seedheads or pollen for them. There is no need to make a special wildlife garden when so many good garden plants are naturally wildlife-friendly. Nowadays, many nursery catalogs indicate which these are, but as a general rule, choose old-fashioned cottage garden plants, such as campanula, and those that are closely related to wild species, such as lythrum. Specially good plants to grow for butterflies include *Sedum spectabile*, scabious and decorative marjorams. Best for bees are symphytum (comfrey), ornamental thyme and lilies. For birds, grow plants with well-filled seedheads, such as bronze fennel, and anything thistlelike or grassy. Some birds also enjoy visiting the flowers of kniphofia and *Euphorbia wulfenii* for nectar. Blend wildlife-friendly perennials into normal borders to bring the garden to life or make a special butterfly bed to draw them to one part of the garden; add buddleia and a mixture of old-fashioned hardy annuals to increase the attraction. As well as bringing in butterflies and bees, perennials also encourage all sorts of beneficial creatures to visit the garden: lacewings, spiders (including tiny money spiders), ladybirds and their larvae and hoverflies all help to keep the garden free from insect pests, as do many insectivorous birds. Encourage wildlife to remain in the garden all year round by delaying your end-of-season clear-up until spring. Birds will feed on seedheads in the fall, and beneficial insects and centipedes, etc., can overwinter in plant debris around the edge of the garden. In time, they will achieve a natural balance that takes care of pest control without chemicals.

Above: Scabiosa caucasica 'Clive Greaves' *prefers chalky well-drained soil. The plants flower all summer and are good for cutting, as well as attracting hordes of butterflies.*

Below: Calamintha nepetoides *has a fresh minty fragrance when the leaves are crushed, and masses of tiny off-white flowers in late summer; it needs a dry sunny spot to flourish.*

Left: Old-fashioned country garden flowers are the best for drawing bees and other insects; here are variegated comfrey, hardy cranesbill and allium.*

Wildlife-friendly perennials

Achillea, Aster,
Campanula lactiflora, C. latiloba
and C. persicifolia,
Decorative marjoram,
Echinacea, Echinops, Eryngium,
Euphorbia wulfenii,
Foeniculum vulgare *'Purpureum'*
(bronze fennel), Kniphofia,
Lilies, Lythrum, *Most grass*
seedheads, Nepeta, *Ornamental*
thyme, Phlox, Pulmonaria,
Scabiosa, Sedum spectabile
Symphytum *(very good for bees)*
Verbena bonariensis

Right: Sedum spectabile, *the butterfly plant, is always smothered in fall. Here, a Painted Lady is enjoying* Sedum spectabile *'Autumn Joy'.*

Below: All the daisy family, especially those with large single flowers and a knobbly central 'boss', are attractive to bees. This is Helenium *'Butterpat'.*

Right: Wild flowers and their close cultivated relatives are always a good draw for insects; this one is Lythrum salicaria *'Feuerkerze', a tall moisture-lover that flowers in mid- to late summer.*

Below: Eryngium tripartitum *has steely-blue flowers on wiry stems with prickly blue-gray hollylike leaves. Plants need a well-drained soil and full sun to thrive. The plants are 'alive' with buzzing bees on warm summer days.*

Above: Verbena bonariensis *is a short-lived perennial that spreads throughout the border by self-seeding gently; plants are tall and have few small leaves, so all you see are the flowers hovering.*

Right: The coneflower (Echinacea purpurea) *has plenty of nectar that butterflies find irresistible. Insects bring the garden to life and add extra color and movement to flowerheads.*

Living carpets

A good perennial border should contain a blend of all the major plant shapes. Dramatic spikes and giant blooms provide 'personality', bushy clumps and airy sprays act as 'fillers' and low, spreading kinds form living carpets in the border. Carpeting plants make up for their lack of glamor by their usefulness. They provide continuity – a living backdrop to the border that sets off more spectacular flowers and links them together visually. They also make very efficient ground cover. As soon as carpeting plants meet and cover the soil in late spring, weed seeds are denied light and so are unable to germinate. Provided no perennial weeds are present, the border will remain virtually weed-free from then until the end of the season. A good covering of low, spreading plants makes it possible to reduce weeding to a couple of sessions in spring, and a late tidy-up in fall. As well as cutting down work, this technique reduces damage to border plants caused by slips with the hoe, or by trying to hand weed a close-planted border; some perennials, such as alstroemeria, are notoriously brittle and stems break off at a touch. The best plants to use for ground cover within a border are those that not only have a naturally low, spreading habit, but are also able to tolerate light shade.

Right: Persicaria bistorta *'Superba' creates a continuous cover of foliage interrupted by short 'pokers' of pink flower. In fall, the foliage takes on warm tints. The plants scramble in amongst shrubs and other perennials, creating a pleasing patchwork picture.*

Above: Brunnera macrophylla *growing under* Betula jacquemontii. *After flowering, in early midsummer, cut back brunnera foliage and dead flower stems close to the ground to get a fresh new crop of foliage and a few late flowers.*

Ground cover perennials for shade

Alchemilla mollis, Bergenia, Brunnera *(Especially variegated forms; good for foliage and seasonal flowers.)*, Campanula persicifolia, Epimedium, Erigeron, Geranium *sp. (Many hardy cranesbills have a long flowering season.)*, Persicaria affinis *and* P. bistorta, Pulmonaria

Right: Alchemilla mollis *(lady's mantle) does not cover the ground by creeping outwards over it as do most carpeting plants. Instead, plants self-seed in most soils to make a dense cover of foliage after a few years. The same effect can be achieved more quickly by planting several plants close together from the start.*

Below: Pulmonaria saccharata *spreads relatively quickly, as offsets form around the parent plant, quickly mature and have 'pups' of their own. Decorative foliage is a feature of this plant, so cut old foliage back close to the ground in midsummer for a fresh crop of young, well-marked leaves.*

Right: Bergenia *spreads slowly by forming clumps. The large evergreen leaves make good weed-smothering cover all year. Plants do well in sun or shade. Divide established clumps in spring or the fall for faster cover.*

Below: Epimedium perralderianum *has beautifully marked heart-shaped leaves that take on deeper fall tints. Leaves may be retained in mild winters, but are shed in cold ones. Spring growth is copper colored.*

Garden giants

There are some situations where plants that stand out alone are called for; perhaps at the water's edge, where a really striking plant is needed to cast dramatic reflections. Some garden styles also demand strongly individual plants, particularly 'jungly' subtropical schemes. These are ideal situations in which to grow the giants of the perennial world. Some of the best for waterside situations are *Darmera peltata* (*Peltiphyllum*) and *Gunnera manicata*. *Darmera* has 12in(30cm)-wide, circular leaves with the stalks attached in the middle, making them look rather like saucers on sticks. The flowers, which look like bright pink asparagus stalks, appear in spring, before the leaves. In fall, the foliage turns orange-red. In a moist border, grow *Sanguisorba obtusa*, a large striking plant with attractively divided leaves and masses of long-stemmed, pink bottlebrush-like flowers from mid- to late summer. It teams well with *Darmera*. *Zantedeschia aethiopica* (arum lily) is another good choice, with its large arrowhead-shaped leaves and white flower spathes; the variety 'Crowborough' is hardiest. It will grow in shallow water at the edge of a pond. In a dry border, choose a relative of seakale, *Crambe cordifolia*. Its huge wiry stems dotted with gypsophila-like flowers appear from a dense clump of enormous crinkly leaves, forming a large mound.

Right: Gunnera manicata *is a truly huge plant with formidably spined stems and leaf-backs. It needs moist soil that never dries out, so is a favorite for waterside planting, where the reflection makes it appear even more impressive.*

Left: *Tough, evergreen and drought-tolerant, the dwarf pampas grass,* Cortaderia pumila, *up to 6ft(1.8m) high, makes a good 'giant' where there is no room for an enormous plant.*

Right: *Crambe cordifolia, a rugged giant with deep roots, is suitable for poor soil as long as it is well-drained and in the sun. It bears airy clouds of perfumed flowers during the summer.*

Left: *Bronze fennel (Foeniculum vulgare purpureum)* is the *ornamental form of the herb fennel. Plants reach a statuesque 6ft(1.8m) with fountains of hairlike leaves and yellow flowers. Birds love the seedheads in fall.*

Above: *Osmunda regalis,* the large and impressive royal fern, forms piles of foliage with coppery highlights that take on bright fall tints. It needs moist, even boggy, conditions.

Below: *The arum lily (Zantedeschia aethiopica)* enjoys moist soil. When planted deeply in mud, it escapes frost. Alternatively, grow it in pots and keep it in a greenhouse in winter.

In winter, bend the dead leaves of gunnera over the crown of the plant to protect it from frost.

Architectural shapes

Make the most of a perennial border by introducing as many distinctive shapes as possible to the mass of bloom. Classic spires of delphinium and lupin, chunky spikes of acanthus, trumpets of lily, the geometric shapes of iris, knobbly thistle heads, such as *Centaurea macrocephala*, flat-topped flowers of *Achillea filipendulina* 'Gold Plate', tiers of phygelius, domes of *Euphorbia wulfenii* and spheres of agapanthus flower add high spots that make flowers stand out as individuals from a busy border. Dot strong architectural shapes throughout a long border to break it up into visual chunks that the onlooker can appreciate better. Or concentrate strong shapes in the center of smaller island beds to form a heart to the display. In smaller borders, look for downscaled versions of classic shapes, such as *Lythrum virgatum* 'The Rocket', which has rosy spikes about 36in(90cm) high, astilbe and *Sedum spectabile,* to achieve similar effects in a small space. Daisy flowers such as echinacea, grasses such as *Imperata cylindrica,* and crocosmia all have strong architectural shapes suitable for smaller spaces. Look out, too, for dwarf varieties of bearded iris, kniphofia and delphinium for large impact on a small scale. In shade, hardy ferns, hostas and ivies combine to make classic foliage gardens. Use architectural plants en masse for impact in special places, perhaps to accentuate a pond or garden ornament. A clump of cimicifuga fills a woodland clearing, while acanthus makes a brilliant backdrop for a classical statue; flank a tall gate or archway with *Macleaya cordata.* Keep to one kind of plant to avoid distracting attention from the main feature.

Below: The dramatic seedheads of Stipa gigantea *erupt from the modest tuft of foliage at the base like a gold and bronze starburst. Stipa needs a sunny spot in well-drained or dry soil.*

Above: Phygelius *has brightly colored tubular flowers in tiers up the stems. It looks superb amongst shrubs and grasses or in a 'hot' border. This is* Phygelius *x* rectus *'African Queen'.*

Left: Ligularia przewalskii *'The Rocket' is well named; its long, lean 6ft(1.8m) flower spikes shoot straight up towards the sun. Provide rich moist or boggy soil.*

Right: Globe artichokes look superb in flower borders. They open out into spectacular purple thistlelike heads that attract butterflies and bees, and also dry well for winter arrangements.

Right: The bottlebrush flowers of Liatris spicata *growing on bold upright stems lined with elegant grassy leaves look as if they were designed by a geometry teacher. Plants need sun and very well-drained soil. They are much appreciated by flower arrangers.*

Suitable plants

Acanthus, Achillea, *esp.* filipendulina *'Gold Plate'*, Agapanthus africanus *or Headbourne Hybrids*, Astilbe, Centaurea macrocephala, Cimicifuga, Crocosmia, Delphinium, Echinacea, Eryngium, Euphorbia wulfenii *and* E. mellifera, *Globe artichoke, Hardy ferns,* Hosta, Imperata cylindrica, Iris, *inc. bearded iris,* Kniphofia, Liatris, Ligularia, *Lily, Lupin,* Lythrum virgatum *'The Rocket'*, Macleaya cordata, Paeonia, Phygelius, Physalis alkekengi, Sedum spectabile, Stipa gigantea

Left: Acanthus has leathery leaves and tough prickly stems topped by regular rows of helmet-shaped flowers that all add a touch of architectural sophistication to borders. Plant in sun.

Perennials for shade

Shady places can be the hardest parts of the garden to plant up colorfully, but a surpising number of perennials in fact do better in shade than in sun. Many are spring-flowering, such as dicentra, hellebores, pulmonaria and polygonatum. In summer, *Euphorbia robbiae*, *Iris foetidissima* and *Geranium phaeum* look good together; team them with shade-loving foliage plants, such as hostas, hardy ferns, lamium and red-leaved forms of bergenia. In winter, the spotted foliage of *Arum italicum* 'Marmoratum' makes a good decorative ground covering. In early spring, well-established clumps have arum lilylike flowers followed by clusters of orange berries. Group any of these together or mix them with shade-tolerant shrubs to make traditional-style borders. Use them in gardens that get little direct sunlight or under a light canopy of trees to add detail to a woodland garden. As a rule, if there is enough light to read by, there is enough for shade-loving perennials to grow in. Increase light in dark areas by painting fences and walls in light pastel colors and use cream-variegated plants, such as *Brunnera macropylla* 'Hadspen Cream' and variegated lamium. Mirrors or water features not only reflect light, add interest and improve conditions for the plants, they also help to make dingy areas of the garden look bigger.

Above: Dicentra spectabilis 'Alba' *(the white form of bleeding heart, also known as lady-in-the-bath) combines well with hostas. The hint of purple is provided by a stray* Euphorbia dulcis 'Chameleon' *seedling.*

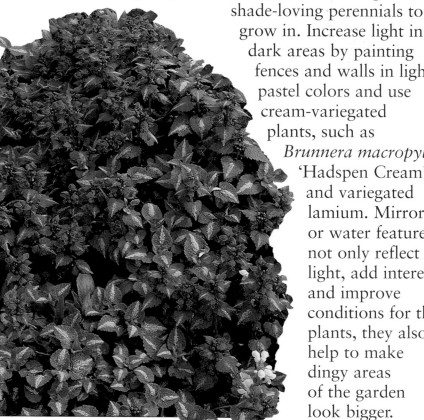

Right: Ornamental deadnettle *(Lamium maculatum) is available in various forms with pink, mauve or white flowers and variegated or silver foliage. It makes very good ground cover in shady positions.*

Left: Astilbes like moist soil and grow well in sun or shade, but since few shade plants provide much color, their plumed flowers are ideal for a shady spot.

Below: Geranium macrorrhizum *is an outstanding shade plant, with its scented spring and early summer flowers followed by distinctive foliage that takes on fall tints.*

Suitable plants

Ajuga, Anemone japonica, Arum italicum '*Marmoratum*', Astilbe, Bergenia, Brunnera, Dicentra, Epilobium angustifolium album, Euphorbia robbiae, Geranium phaeum, Geum rivale, *Hardy ferns*, Helleborus, Hosta, Iris foetidissima, Lamium, Liriope muscari, Lysimachia nummularia '*Aurea*', Polemonium, Polygonatum, Primula auricula *and* vulgaris, Pulmonaria, Symphytum, Tricytris, Viola odorata

Below: Toad lilies, such as this Tricyrtis hirta 'Variegata', are far more beautiful than their common name suggests. They are good and unusual plants for light shade, but much loved by slugs and snails.

Perennials for damp places

Damp-loving perennials are ideal for planting in 'difficult' badly drained ground, a stream or ditch, or to create authentic waterside planting around garden ponds; some even suit bog garden conditions. Damp-loving perennials naturally associate well together, and many have spectacular flowers or foliage, so group them according to size to create dramatic displays. At the smaller end of the scale are plants such as hostas, astilbes, *Mimulus* x *burnettii* and *Lysimachia nummularia* 'Aurea', a form of creeping Jenny with gold leaves like rows of gold coins strung in rows. In the medium range – about 24-36in (60-90cm) high – are several species of iris, including the water irises, *Iris laevigata* (good for bog gardens or in shallow water in a pond edge), the Japanese water irises, *Iris ensata*, and *Iris sibirica*, both good for damp borders. Also in this size range are *Lobelia cardinalis* 'Queen Victoria', which has purple leaves and cardinal-red flowers, *Lythrum virgatum* 'The Rocket', which has narrow spires of rosy-mauve flowers, and the candelabra primulas (*P. japonica* and *pulverulenta*) with their striking 'tiered' flowers. In the tall group come *Lysimachia* (loosestrife), *Cimicifuga* (bugbane), *Lythrum* (purple loosestrife), *Rodgersia* and *Ligularia*, all great for damp wild gardens as well as informal borders. *Sanguisorba obtusa* is particularly spectacular, with large pink bottlebrushlike flowers in late summer and fall. Even in a small garden a few tall plants look good towards the back of a boggy border, but avoid leaving them unchecked for several years or they can swamp smaller species. Treat the skunk cabbage (*Lysichiton americanum*) as a specimen plant to grow in isolation, perhaps at the water's edge. It is a very dramatic plant, with large leaves and yellow arum-lily flowers in spring.

Improving the soil

Protect plants that enjoy damp soil from drying out at the roots in summer by mulching in spring with well-rotted organic matter such as garden compost. If an artificial bog garden will not naturally remain wet all year round, excavate the area to a depth of at least 24in(60cm) and line the base with pond liner or 2in(5cm) of clay puddled with water and trodden down well. Fill with clay-loam topsoil mixed with well-rotted organic matter. If watering becomes necessary, the moisture will be retained.

Above: Iris sibirica *cultivars all enjoy moist but not waterlogged soil and a sunny spot. Plants reach 36in(90cm) high, and clumps rarely need dividing. This cultivar is 'Tropic Night'.*

Below: Marsh marigold grows wild by streams and in wet meadows. Use it in wild gardens or beside a pond. Various cultivated forms are available, including some good doubles.

Below: Many primula species suit moist soil; choose P. florindae *(giant Himalayan cowslip) and candelabra primulas* (P. pulverulenta, japonica and beesiana). *All hybridize freely.*

Left: Lobelia cardinalis *'Victoria' (cardinal flower) is a great favorite, with its purple foliage and tall spires of bright red flower in mid- to late summer.*

Right: Purple loosestrife (Lythrum salicaria) *makes a giant of a plant for a large damp border or wild garden pondside. It self-seeds very freely, so is best deadheaded after flowering.*

Carex elata *'Aurea' (Bowles' golden sedge)*

Below: Carex elata *'Aurea', (Bowles' golden sedge),* Houttuynia cordata *'Chameleon' and creeping Jenny (Lysimachia nummularia) make a good plant association for moist soil or pondside planting.*

Houttuynia cordata *'Chameleon'*

Lysimachia nummularia *'Aurea' (creeping Jenny)*

*Above: Skunk cabbage (*Lysichiton americanum*) is so-called due to the unpleasant smell of the flowers, but it is a very striking plant measuring 36in(90cm) or more across.*

Dry borders

In regions with low summer rainfall, or on light sandy or chalky soils that dry out quickly, many popular perennials find conditions too dry for their liking. Soil improvement is vital, so when making a new bed be sure to dig in as much organic matter as possible. Because organic matter decomposes so quickly in light soil, it is not so necessary to use well-rotted manure or garden compost; partially rotted material will last longer in the soil. Even so, after the new bed has been planted up, regular 'top-ups' of organic matter will keep the soil fertile, so mulch twice yearly, in spring and fall. On very fast-drying soils, it is worth digging water-retaining gel crystals into the top layer when preparing the soil. Choose naturally drought-tolerant perennial species. As a rule, plants with silver, waxy or prickly leaves, such as artemisia, *Sedum spectabile* and eryngium, are the most drought-tolerant, as are those such as agapanthus, whose natural home is hot dry and sunny. However, even drought-tolerant plants are only 'safe' once well established. When first planted on dry soil, water them throughout their first summer.

Right: Eryngium maritimum *is ideal for coastal gardens. It tolerates wind and salt and grows in sand and pebbles. Plants grow up to 18in(45cm) high.*

Below: Sisyrinchium striatum *has upright 24in(60cm) flower spikes in early summer. It seeds itself into the most inhospitable cracks and crevices, yet always blooms well.*

Left: Agapanthus is a good plant for a hot dry sunny bed or a large container. Protect it from frost, and in cold climates bring it under cover for the winter. This cultivar is 'Purple Cloud'.

Self-seeding perennials

If watering newly planted perennials is a problem, grow varieties that self-seed, such as Alchemilla mollis, Linaria purpurea and Verbena bonariensis. Plant pot-grown plants in flower and keep them well watered until they shed seed. Allow the seedlings to develop where they grow; simply weed out unwanted seedlings – do not transplant them. Self-sown seedlings make a much more efficient root system and develop into far more drought-proof plants than any that have been transplanted from elsewhere in the garden.

Above: Artemisia 'Powis Castle' is a non-flowering form, so the filigree foliage remains a feature all summer. It associates well with flowering herbs, here Origanum laevigatum.

Suitable plants

Acanthus, Agapanthus,
Alchemilla mollis, Alstroemeria,
Artemisia, *esp.* 'Powis Castle',
Bearded iris, Centranthus,
Echinops ritro, Eryngium,
Euphorbia mellifera, E. wulfenii,
Kniphofia, Linaria purpurea,
Nepeta, Penstemon,
Sedum spectabile
Sisyrinchium striatum,
Stachys lanata,
Verbascum bombyciferum

Above: *Valerian (Centranthus ruber) will grow in rocks or rubble, on stone walls, or in cracks between paving slabs and still need no watering. Plants self-seed gently around.*

Right: *Lambs ears, Stachys lanata, makes a carpet of furry silver foliage, punctuated in summer by tall fluff-clad spikes of pink flower. This cultivar is 'Silver Carpet'.*

Spring-flowering perennials

Herbaceous borders are traditionally at their peak in summer, yet there are plenty of spring-flowering kinds that are useful for getting the season off to a colorful start. In a small garden, it is best to create several spring 'cameos', teaming spring bulbs and early-flowering perennials with perhaps a few shrubs. Grouping spring-flowering species together makes more impact than dotting them around the garden, and by keeping them separate from summer plants, the focus shifts naturally around the garden throughout the year – a good way of adding variety and interest to a small space. However, in large gardens, it is feasible to make borders large enough to accommodate both spring and summer perennials without the borders looking 'thin' during either season. For best effect, mix the two evenly together throughout the border, with spring species towards the front. In this way, the attractive foliage of plants such as pulmonaria acts as a foil to later flowers, and will not be smothered by fast-growing, rampant summer plants. If the border is underplanted with naturalized spring bulbs, use groups of early-flowering perennials such as brunnera to complement them; they associate very nicely together.

Bulb foliage

To avoid borders looking untidy while daffodil foliage dies down, grow spreading plants, such as hardy cranesbills (Geranium species), in front of them to mask the foliage. Use herbaceous clematis such as C. integrifolia 'Rosea' to conceal bluebell foliage with a carpet of flowers. Alternatively, avoid planting bulbs with large or long-lasting leaves, and plant dwarf bulbs instead. To avoid damaging bulbs when hoeing a herbaceous border, either plant them in distinct groups and mark the spot with a permanent plant label, or plant deeper than usual – well below hoe depth; this will not harm the bulbs.

Below: Bergenias such as this cheerful 'Ballawley' provide winter and spring color. In some varieties, the leathery evergreen foliage takes on purplish or metallic tints during cold weather.

Above: Brunnera macrophylla makes good ground cover until summer. Cut down foliage and dead flower stems close to the ground in midsummer.

Above: Doronicum is one of the first perennials to flower; team it with daffodils and pulmonaria for a pretty display. Doronicum grows in sun or light shade and most soils. Divide the plants every third year and grow them in groups for the best effect.

Above: Dicentra spectabilis *is brilliant for light dappled shade, but is happy in sun if the soil stays sufficiently cool and moist. If grown among shrubs, it uses the branches to support its rather lax stems. Plants reach 48in(120cm).*

Right: Corydalis flexuosa *is popular for well-drained, humus-rich borders in light shade. It suits an informal woodland style border, but also looks good beneath shrubs. Team it with* Anemone blanda *or* A. nemorosa.

Left: *The spotted leaves of pulmonaria make a good background for the yellow flowers of* Ranunculus ficaria *(cultivated celandines) and* Omphalodes cappadocica *'Starry Eyes'. All these plants enjoy cool moist soil and shade, and when left undisturbed will ramble gently around, creating an informal patchwork of color in the garden.*

Suitable plants

Bergenia, Brunnera,
Caltha, Corydalis flexuosa,
Dicentra, Epimedium,
Erysimum, Euphorbia,
Geranium macrorrhizum,
Geum, Helleborus,
Lamium, Polygonatum
(Solomon's seal),
Pulmonaria, Trollius

81

Summer choices

Traditional favorites, such as lupins, delphiniums and achillea, are the mainstay of many perennial beds. They are useful in mixed borders to provide summer flowers after the main shrub flowering season is over, or in new shrub or rose borders to fill the space between plants for the first few years until the shrubs grow up. Plants such as bearded iris, peony, *Campanula persicifolia* and oriental poppy, flower at the start of summer and can leave gaps in the border when their main season has finished, so make sure their neighbors provide later color to make up for them. Flowers such as lupin, astrantia and delphinium often flower for a second time if cut down immediately after the main flowering. Cut the flowered stems back to just above the cluster of leaves near the base of the plant. Other plants also benefit from early cutting back; these include variegated perennials, such as variegated astrantia, which become plain green as the season progresses, and plants that often develop mildewed leaves after flowering, such as pulmonaria. Trim them just above ground level.

Left: Ornamental knotweeds are extremely useful ground-covering perennials that flower from midsummer until the first frosts. Many have colorful fall foliage tints. This is Persicaria amplexicaulis 'Firetail'.

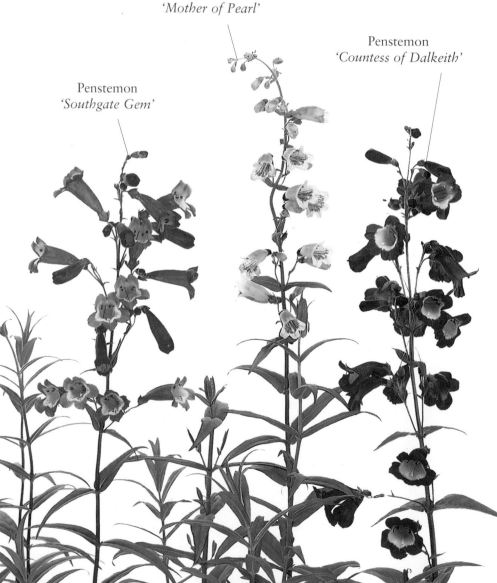

Penstemon 'Mother of Pearl'

Penstemon 'Countess of Dalkeith'

Penstemon 'Southgate Gem'

Above: Penstemon and achillea create continuity between the antirrhinums and roses in a red border. Diluting the flower colors with green and purple foliage creates a coordinated effect.

Right: Penstemons flower until the first frosts, but are not reliably frost hardy. Take cuttings in late summer to overwinter indoors.

Left: *Globe thistles like well-drained soil and a sunny situation, and are happy even in poor sandy or chalky soil. This is* Echinops bannaticus. *The tall blooms attract moths in the early evening.*

Right: *Herbaceous peonies, such as this 'Gleam of Light', produce spectacular blooms, but they flower for just a few weeks in early summer, so surround them with later flowers to avoid leaving a gap in the border display.*

Summer perennials

Achillea, Astilbe, Astrantia, Campanula, Centaurea, Chrysanthemum maximum, Clematis durandii *and* C. integrifolia *'Rosea',* Coreopsis, Coronaria, Crocosmia, Delphinium, Dianthus, Diascia, Dictamnus, Echinacea, Echinops, Erigeron, Gaillardia, Geranium, Gypsophila, Hemerocallis, Heuchera, Iris sibirica *and* bearded iris, Ligularia, Lilium, Lupin, Lychnis, Nepeta, Paeonia, Papaver orientale, Penstemon, Persicaria, Salvia *x* sylvestris, Scabiosa, Sidalcea, Thalictrum, Tradescantia

Right: *Lupins need plenty of sun and very well-drained but rich soil. Plants live longest in lime-free soil. They grow to about 48in(1.2m) high and 24in(60cm) across. Many have flowers with a two-tone effect, such as this cultivar, 'Poached Salmon'.*

Right: Astrantia is known as Hattie's pincushion, due to the shape and texture of the flowerheads. Most have white, greenish or pale pink flowers, although there are a few deep pink or nearly red forms. This is 'Hadspen Blood'. Plants flower all summer.

Below: In a well-drained sunny spot, diascias, such as this 'Joyce's Choice', flower from early midsummer to fall. Plants live longest when grown on raised beds or rock gardens, but also do well in tubs and borders. Provide winter protection in cold regions.

Right: Newer cultivars of achillea flower more prolifically and with colors in the pink and red range, as well as yellow. These are 'Coronation Gold' and 'Smiling Queen'. Achilleas are good for cutting and drying.

Left: From early to late summer, the ferny foliage and flat heads of achillea flowers contrast well with upright or spiky shapes in the border. Yellow cultivars, such as this 'Gold Plate', are old favorites.

Right: For a first-class display of delphiniums, mulch them heavily in spring and liquid feed throughout the summer. Protect from slugs and snails, and support the stems with tall stakes as they develop.

Above: Potentilla atrosanguinea makes neat, ground-covering mounds 24in(60cm) across and 18in(45cm) high. Some cultivars have bronze foliage. Plant in a well-drained, sunny spot as part of a bright color scheme.

Below: The large hand-sized leaves of heuchera make handsome ground cover in sun or light shade. Green-leaved cultivars have red flowers; plum-leaved ones, such as this 'Palace Purple', have pink or white flowers.

Left: Regular deadheading is the secret to keeping perennials with a long flowering season constantly in bloom. However, even with flowers such as delphiniums, it is worth cutting off the dead heads when the flowers are over, to encourage a second, late, light crop of flowers.

Filling the late-summer gap

By late summer, perennial borders often look a bit jaded as the majority of classic summer flowers go over. The most reliable way to avoid boring borders in late summer is to include a good sprinkling of natural late-starters throughout the garden. These include Japanese anemones, *Aster* x *frikartii*, phlox, agapanthus, solidago (golden rod), *Macleaya cordata*, cimicifuga, and several varieties of kniphofia. Also guaranteed to make a good late show are late-summer classics, such as Michaelmas daisies and New England asters (which are less prone to mildew), plus many late daisies, such as rudbeckia, helenium, *Chrysanthemum rubellum* and helianthus. Slightly more unusual is phygelius, which has elegant tiered heads of brightly colored flowers, perfect for a sunny spot amongst shrubs. In light shade or a woodland garden, choose the toad lily *(Tricyrtis)* with its small, mauve-spotted lily flowers, and *Kirengeshoma palmata*, which has tall stems of vine-leaf-like foliage topped by yellow flowers. The unusual *Liriope muscari*, or lilyturf, has squat lilylike foliage and short spikes of mauve-purple flowers. Many late summer flowers begin flowering now, and depending on the weather, may continue well into the fall, signalling the start of a gradual transformation to a new season.

Below: Red hot pokers (Kniphofia) *are not all red; some have yellow or even greenish-cream flowers. Various small garden birds feed on their nectar. They are all plants for a hot sunny spot with well-drained soil.*

Below: The pincushion flowers of Knautia macedonica *are an unusual deep crimson, growing on neat plants 24in(60cm) tall and wide. Grow it in well-drained soil in a sunny spot.*

Left: Aster *x* frikartii *'Mönch' is one of the best perennial asters, as it begins to flower earlier than Michaelmas daisies and has a flowering season about twice as long – from midsummer to fall. It is also much less prone to mildew.*

Left: Japanese anemones flower in sun or light shade and grow from 24-48in (60-120cm) tall according to variety. These are Anemone 'Honorine Jobert' and 'Prinz Heinrich' (pink).

Right: 'Headbourne Hybrids' are one of the most reliable agapanthus strains for regions with cold winters. Plants flower well despite poor summers, but do best in a well-drained sunny border.

Below: Phlox paniculata 'Mary Fox' and Phygelius x rectus 'Devil's Tears' make a good combination. The color of the phygelius flowers picks out the color of the central 'eye' of the phlox.

Liriope muscari *grows 12in(30cm) high and slowly spreads to cover a wide area.*

Below: Liriope muscari *is an unusual perennial that enjoys dry shady borders, although it also grows well in damper and sunnier situations as long as these are reasonably well drained.*

Long flowering

Given particularly good care, some summer perennials, such as diascia, penstemon and astrantia, can continue flowering into late summer. For this to happen, it is vital that plants have good growing conditions: enough water, plenty of feed and a deep mulch to keep their roots cool, plus summer weather that is not too hot. Regular dead-heading is also essential to stop plants setting seed; if this happens they do not produce the new shoots that will carry a late flush of flowers.

Late-season impact

Fall-flowering perennials have really come into their own in recent years. There are not many of them; look for schizostylis, *Sedum spectabile*, *Kniphofia galpinii* and *Physalis alkekengi franchetii* and really make the most of them. All make displays that do not start until fall and continue until the first severe gales or hard frosts. These late-peaking plants are particularly valuable when hot dry summers advance the usual summer displays and bring them to a prematurely early end. In such seasons, even late-summer perennials can start flowering in midsummer. In small gardens, where there is not enough room to grow the kind of trees that provide traditional fall color, late perennial flowers can more than compensate. Group them with late-summer flowers to make seasonal cameos, or team them with shrubs that take on fall tints, such as some of the Japanese maples, underplanted with colchicums and fall crocus. In a large border, blend fall flowers in amongst summer and late-summer perennials, so that the whole border gradually changes throughout the season. Or use late perennials to signal the start of a new season, planting them with winter-flowering shrubs, such as witch hazel, wintersweet and winter jasmine, with a foreground of bergenia, whose huge leaves take on red or purple tints in cold weather.

Suitable plants

Aster amellus *cultivars*,
A. novae-angliae,
A pringlei *'Monte Cassino'*,
Chrysanthemum rubellum *sp.,*
Kniphofia galpinii
(rare: flowers in mid-fall),
Michaelmas diasies,
Physalis alkekengi franchetii
(lanternlike seedpods in fall),
Schizostylis, Sedum spectabile

Below: Sedum spectabile *cultivars are available with terracotta and rose pink flowers, also white and nearly red. All attract huge numbers of butterflies in late summer and fall.*

Above: *In the fall, the large seedpods of Iris foetidissima split open to reveal rows of red pealike seeds that are particularly striking when they are rimmed with frost.*

Sedum spectabile
'Stardust'

Sedum spectabile
'Meteor'

Sedum spectabile
'Brilliant'

Above: A very few red hot pokers, including this Kniphofia galpinii, flower late and continue until the frosts. Plants are worth seeking out for their valuable end of year display.

Above: Schizostylis coccinea *is a member of the gladiolus family. Unlike gladioli though, schizostylis flower late in the year, enjoy damp soil and grow only about 15in(38cm) high. Give them a sunny spot.*

Right: Aster amellus *is a good alternative to Michaelmas daisy for low-maintenance or organic gardens. The plants are shorter and stronger than Michaelmas daisy so need no staking; neither do they suffer from mildew, so spraying is not necessary.*

Above: Chinese lantern (Physalis alkekengi franchetii) *looks rather dull in summer, but erupts into fountains of brilliant orange-red lanterns (actually seedpods) in the fall. The plants can be dried for winter arrangements.*

Index to Plants

Page numbers in **bold** indicate major references. Numbers in *italics* indicate panels, captions and annotations. Other text entries are shown in normal type.

Credits

The majority of the photographs featured in this book have been taken by Neil Sutherland and are © Colour Library Books. The publishers wish to thank the following photographers for providing additional photographs, credited here by page number and position on the page, i.e. (B)Bottom, (T)Top, (C)Center, (BL)Bottom left, etc.

Blooms of Bressingham: 62(TR)
Eric Crichton: 17(TR), 24(B), 26(B), 34(CR), 35(BL), 37(TR, BR), 38(BR), 39(BR), 40(B), 44(BR), 51(TR, BL), 55(TL), 58(BR), 59(BR), 60(BR), 63(BL), 70(BR), 71(BR), 72(BC), 75(T, BR), 77(TR, BR), 79(TL, BR), 80(BL), 81(TR), 86(BL), 89(TC)
John Glover: 23(CL), 27(T), 35(TC, TR), 37(TL), 38(T), 39(TR), 52(T), 54(BL), 55(TR), 56(BR), 61(BL), 68(T), 69(TR), 72(T, BR), 79(TR), 82(BL) 86(TR, C), 89(R)
Andrew Lawson: 25(TR), 58(T), 59(TL, TR), 60(BL), 63(TR)
S & O Mathews: 21(BL), 26(T), 27(B), 29(TR), 31(TC), 34(BR), 56(T, BL), 57(TC, BR), 58(BL), 62(BL), 63(TL), 64(CB), 65(BL), 67(TR), 69(BR), 71(TR), 73(TC), 74(L), 76(BR), 81(B), 89(BL)
Clive Nichols: 24(T), 33(TR), 41(TL), 45(T), 46(T), 47(BC), 53(BR), 54(BR), 69(BL), 74(R), 78(T), 83(TL), 88(BL)
Photos Horticultural: 63(BR)
Derek St. Romaine Photography: 61(TC, BR)
Geoffrey Rogers: Half-title page, Copyright page, 11, 13(TC, BR), 28(T), 29(TL, BL), 30(BL, T), 32(T), 33(BL), 34(BL), 35(TL, BR), 38(BL), 40(T), 41(TR, CR, BL, BR), 44(BL), 45(BL, BC, BR), 46(B), 47(TL, BR), 55(BL), 59(CL), 66(BR), 67(CR, BL), 70(BL), 73(BR), 75(BL), 77(TL), 78(BL), 80(T, BR), 81(TL), 83(TR), 84(TL, BR), 86(BR), 87(TL), 88(BR), 89(TL)
Valley Green: 60(TR), 61(TR), 62(BR)

Acknowledgments

The publishers would like to thank the following people and organizations for their help during the production of this book; Diana Grenfell at Apple Court , Lymington, Hampshire; Hazel Kennelly and all the staff at Coblands Herbaceous Unit, Ivy Hatch, Kent; Peter Dench; Keith Backhouse at Hadlow College, Kent; Hall Place Gardens and Nursery, Bexley, Kent; Mark Buchele at Merriments, Hurst Green, East Sussex; Murrells Nursery, Pulborough, West Sussex; Terry and Lesley Neale of Neales Aquatic Nurseries, Fawkham, Kent; Rosie and Robin Lloyd at Pots and Pithoi, Turners Hill, West Sussex; June Crowe at Rose Cottage, Hartley, Kent; Stapeley Water Gardens, Nantwich, Cheshire; Sarah Wain at Edward James Foundation, West Dean Gardens, West Sussex.